Stop, Think, Act

Stop, Think, Act: Integrating Self-Regulation in the Early Childhood Classroom offers early childhood teachers the latest research and a wide variety of hands-on activities to help children learn and practice self-regulation techniques. Self-regulation in early childhood leads to strong academic performance, helps students form healthy friendships, and gives them the social and emotional resources they need to face high-stress situations throughout life.

The book takes you through everything you need to know about using self-regulation principles during circle time, in literacy and math instruction, and during gross motor and outdoor play. Each chapter includes a solid research base as well as practical, developmentally appropriate games, songs, and strategies that you can easily incorporate in your own classroom. With *Stop, Think, Act*, you'll be prepared to integrate self-regulation into every aspect of the school day.

Megan M. McClelland is the Katherine E. Smith Healthy Children and Families Professor in Human Development and Family Sciences at Oregon State University. Her research focuses on optimizing children's development, especially as it relates to children's self-regulation and school readiness, including links between self-regulation and academic achievement from early childhood to adulthood, recent advances in measuring self-regulation, and intervention efforts to improve these skills in young children.

Shauna L. Tominey is an associate research scientist at the Yale Center for Emotional Intelligence. As the Director of Early Childhood Programming and Teacher Education, her work focuses on developing and implementing programs aimed at improving social and emotional outcomes for children and families.

D1569731

Stop, Think, Act

Integrating Self-Regulation in the Early Childhood Classroom

Megan M. McClelland and Shauna L. Tominey

Routledge
Taylor & Francis Group

NEW YORK AND LONDON

First published 2016
by Routledge
711 Third Avenue, New York, NY 10017

and by Routledge
2 Park Square, Milton Park, Abingdon, Oxon, OX14 4RN

Routledge is an imprint of the Taylor & Francis Group, an informa business

Library of Congress Cataloging-in-Publication Data
McClelland, Megan.
  Stop, think, act : integrating self-regulation in the early childhood classroom /
by Megan M. McClelland and Shauna L. Tominey.
    pages cm
  Includes bibliographical references and index.
  1. Early childhood education.   2. Early childhood education—Activity programs.
3. Motivation in education.   4. Self-control in children.   5. Classroom
management.   I. Tominey, Shauna.   II. Title.
  LB1139.23.M44 2016
  372.21—dc23
  2015011716

ISBN: 978-0-415-74522-2 (hbk)
ISBN: 978-0-415-74523-9 (pbk)
ISBN: 978-1-315-79805-9 (ebk)

Typeset in Utopia
by Apex CoVantage, LLC

MM: This book is dedicated to my husband and children, who are my source of inspiration. Thank you for helping me balance it all!

ST: To my husband and daughter for filling my days with love, support, and inspiration.

Contents ● ● ● ● ●

Contents

Tables ●●●●●

Acknowledgments ● ● ● ● ●

There are many special people in our lives who have shaped our personal and professional paths and helped make this book possible. Thank you to all of our mentors, colleagues, family, and friends, who have influenced our work and supported us through this endeavor. We would like to acknowledge a few special individuals here.

MM: I would like to thank my co-author, Shauna Tominey, who has been a driving force behind this project. Her creativity, intelligence, and passion are truly amazing to see. I would also like to thank my dad, Charles McClelland, for helping us get this project going in the first place. And a special thanks to the rest of my family (Mom, stepparents, and sisters) for keeping me sane, giving me a sense of humor, and being such an incredible support! And finally, to my husband, Roger, for always believing in me and being there for me. I love you!

ST: I cannot give enough thanks to my co-author, Megan McClelland, who has been an inspiring mentor, colleague, and friend. My family also deserves special recognition—my dad for being a role model as a lifelong educator and writer, my mom for being my biggest cheerleader, and my sister and her family for giving me plenty to write about. I also want to acknowledge my friends and colleagues who have greatly influenced my thinking through their work bettering the lives of children and families, including Melissa Thomas and Sharon Shapses. Many thanks to the children in my life who inspire me to do the work that I do, especially Winter, Lily, Leo, and Juliet. And of course, I would not have been able to complete this project without a tremendous amount of support from my husband, Colin. I love you!

1

●●●●●

Self-Regulation in Early Childhood

Ben and Max are playing together during free-play time at their pre-school. Both are very interested in a new kitchen that just arrived and are discussing cooking breakfast. Ben gets out the ingredients for pancakes, and Max starts to get out pans and cooking utensils. Everything is going well until Max puts on the only classroom apron and announces that he is the cook. Unfortunately, Ben wants to be the cook too and the two boys begin an aggressive tug-of-war over the apron. Their teacher, Ms. Lopez, steps in and calmly suggests that they can both be cooks and take turns wearing the apron. Before she has finished talking, Max hits Ben on the head with a wooden spoon and Ben starts to cry. Feeling frustrated, Ms. Lopez pictures herself snapping at Max, saying, "Look what you did now!" but instead takes a deep breath and addresses the conflict between the two boys calmly.

This scenario demonstrates a breakdown in self-regulation for Max and Ben. For Ms. Lopez, this scenario demonstrates a self-regulation success! In this situation, Max and Ben had difficulty with self-regulation when they began fighting over the apron rather than using words or other methods to come to a compromise. Max also showed difficulties when he was unable to stop and listen to Ms. Lopez's words before reacting and hitting Ben with a spoon. Fortunately, Ms. Lopez did not let her frustration get the better of her, but was able to stop herself from snapping to calmly guide Max through steps to think about his actions, apologize to his friend, ask if he was okay, and make amends. This scenario is just one example of situations like this that arise again and again in early childhood classrooms.

Children are repeatedly called upon to use self-regulation throughout the day in large and small group settings. Children who struggle with self-regulation skills have difficulty building and maintaining positive relationships, paying attention, following directions, and controlling unwanted impulses, all of which impact learning (Blair & Diamond, 2008; Diamond, 2010; McClelland & Cameron, 2011).

In fact, when asked, kindergarten teachers report that being able to pay attention and follow directions are the skills most helpful to children when they start kindergarten (Rimm-Kaufman, Pianta, & Cox, 2000)—in other words, being able to demonstrate self-regulation is key. Without adequate self-regulation, children may struggle socially and academically and, as a result, gradually disengage from school and learning. Alarmingly, there is evidence that this process begins as early as the end of kindergarten (Blair & Diamond, 2008; Ladd, Birch, & Buhs, 1999). Because early academic skills lay the foundation for later success, children who fall behind during early childhood or early elementary school because of difficulties with self-regulation may face achievement gaps that are difficult or even impossible to overcome.

The good news is that there is plenty of evidence that self-regulation can be taught, practiced, and improved. This is important because children with strong self-regulation have higher levels of classroom functioning, school adjustment, motivation, and engagement in learning (Denham & Weissberg, 2004; Zsolnai, 2002). Children with strong self-regulation abilities also have better relationships with teachers and peers and an easier time in school (Eisenberg, Eggum, Sallquist, & Edwards, 2010; Ladd & Dinella, 2009). Although early childhood teacher education programs often include self-regulation as an important developmental topic, few programs adequately provide teachers with the specific skills and strategies they need to promote children's self-regulation in the classroom (Tominey & Rivers, 2012). The struggles that many children have with self-regulation in early childhood, combined with a lack of information on how to promote these skills, likely contribute to the high rates of expulsion at the preschool age—three times the combined rate for students in grades K-12 (Gilliam & Shabar, 2006). Finding easy ways to integrate self-regulation practice in early childhood is critical to ensuring that early childhood education teachers feel confident managing the many self-regulation challenges that arise on a daily basis and ensuring all children receive the high-quality early education they need for success.

● ● ● ● ●

Using This Book: Promoting Self-Regulation in Your Own Classroom

A growing body of research highlights the importance of self-regulation for short- and long-term social and academic success (McClelland, Ponitz, Messersmith, & Tominey, 2010). With so much research pointing to self-regulation as foundational for school readiness, our aim in writing this book was to provide you, our readers—early childhood educators and professionals working with young children and families—with a resource to support your ability to effectively promote self-regulation in your classroom or early learning setting. By sharing a combination of research, practical tips, and strategies, we hope to provide you with a solid foundation in research on the importance of self-regulation as well as concrete ways to embed self-regulation into your classroom curriculum and routines through games, activities, songs, and more.

This book includes a summary of recent research on self-regulation, including:

- The "hot" and "cool" components of self-regulation
- How self-regulation develops
- Why early childhood is a critical period for promoting self-regulation
- Best practices for promoting self-regulation in early childhood
- The relationship between self-regulation and academic achievement
- Strategies for engaging families in children's self-regulation development and growth
- How self-regulation is measured and assessed
- And much more!

Each chapter combines research with practice, using examples and anecdotes, learning checkpoints, and teaching tips that you can begin using in the classroom immediately or bookmark for another time. Spread throughout the book are "Activity Breaks" with specific games and activities aimed at promoting self-regulation throughout the preschool day. Although it may seem beneficial to turn straight to the "Activity Breaks," we encourage you to read this book in its entirety to gain a solid foundation of the work and evidence that support these ideas. Each chapter provides information that will help shape your knowledge of self-regulation across the developmental domains and contexts of children's lives, enabling you to use our suggestions more effectively and create your own activities to help children practice these important skills. The last chapter of the book, Chapter 9, provides a list of resources corresponding with each chapter, including recommendations for children's books, music, websites, and much more to support your ability to integrate self-regulation into your classroom. We hope that you will find the research and practical activities in this book useful and easy to integrate into your current teaching strategies and classroom curriculum.

In this first chapter, we lay the foundation for the remaining chapters by providing a definition for self-regulation, examples of how self-regulation might look in early childhood settings, and ideas to help you expand your toolbox of self-regulation activities for use in your classroom.

● ● ● ● ●

What Is Self-Regulation?

We define self-regulation as the conscious control of thoughts, behaviors, and emotions (McClelland et al., 2010). Simply put, self-regulation is the ability to stop, think, and *then* act. Another term that you might hear that is closely related to self-regulation is "executive function." Executive function includes three components: *attentional (or cognitive) flexibility, inhibitory control,* and *working memory* (Garon, Bryson, & Smith, 2008). Self-regulation is the ability to integrate all three aspects of executive function into behavior (McClelland et al., 2010). At face value, the components of executive function may sound complex, but we hope to make them easier to understand through examples (see Table 1.1).

Attentional Flexibility

Attentional flexibility is the ability to pay attention and focus on a task and the ability to switch attention away from that task when needed (Rueda, Posner, & Rothbart, 2005). For example, picture Mia painting happily at the easel. When her teacher begins singing the cleanup song, Mia places her picture on the drying rack, hangs up her smock, and joins her class on the rug. In this example, Mia demonstrates attentional flexibility in several ways. First, she paid attention to the task at hand (painting at the easel). Second, she switched her attention away from painting and refocused her attention to cleaning alongside her classmates when her teacher provided a cue that it was time to clean up.

Table 1.1 Examples of Executive Function Constructs

Executive function construct	How this looks
Attentional/cognitive flexibility	• Paying attention
	• Listening to and following directions
	• Switching focus from one task to another
	• Ignoring distractions
Working memory	• Using short-term memory
	• Remembering single and multi-step directions
	• Recalling and recognizing facts, lessons, or instructions
Inhibitory control	• Controlling impulses
	• Stopping one behavior and choosing another more appropriate action
	• Calming down when upset
	• Taking turns
	• Waiting/delaying gratification

Working Memory

Working memory is the ability to mentally hold and process information (Gathercole, 2008). In preschool, children are continually being asked to use their working memory to remember instructions and rules and to follow directions. Information that children receive may be simple (e.g., a one-step direction) or complex (e.g., multi-step directions). For example, when Gabby arrives at school, she remembers that she must wash her hands before playing—a one-step direction. In another example, Jordan follows through with a complex set of instructions when he uses his working memory to help him remember to hang up his coat after playing outside, go straight to the bathroom, wash his hands, and join his classmates at the table for snack.

Inhibitory Control

Inhibitory control is the ability to stop an impulse and select another more adaptive response in its place (Dowsett & Livesey, 2000). For example, when Emma raises her hand and waits to be called on rather than shouting out a response, she is demonstrating inhibitory control. When Theo stops himself from hitting a friend who has just taken his toy and instead says, "That's mine! Please give it back!" he is also demonstrating inhibitory control.

● ● ● ● ●

Learning Checkpoint

1. How would you describe *attentional flexibility*, *working memory*, and *inhibitory control* in your own words? How do these concepts relate to one another and how are they different from one another?
2. Can you come up with a specific example of how each might look in the classroom?

● ● ● ● ●

Executive Function and Self-Regulation: Putting It All Together

These three executive function skills are distinct from one another, but they often go hand in hand. For instance, in order to use inhibitory control skills, a child needs working memory to keep in mind the appropriate alternate response to use instead of an impulse. To remember this alternate response, the child must have paid attention to the information in the first place. Let's put this together in an example.

Sophie had a strong impulse to push other children who stood in her way. Her teacher, Mr. Rob, worked hard to catch Sophie in these moments and reminded her to say, "Can you move, please?" and wait for her friend to move out of the way rather than pushing. As the year went on, Mr. Rob watched proudly as Sophie used her words more often and pushed less frequently.

In the foregoing scenario, Sophie uses all three executive function skills to develop a new pattern of behavior. She paid *attention* to Mr. Rob when he modeled the appropriate behavior and language to use with her friends. She was able to remember that information by keeping it in her *working memory*, and ultimately she was able to recall it as she exhibited *inhibitory control*, stopping herself from pushing and using language instead. In this example, Sophie was practicing and demonstrating self-regulation. What times of day and in what other ways do you see self-regulation emerging in your classroom? See Table 1.2 for examples of ways that self-regulation might emerge in an early childhood classroom.

Table 1.2 Examples of Self-Regulation in the Early Childhood Classroom

Group Size	Activity	Ways that Children Might Demonstrate Self-Regulation
Large group	Group/circle time or morning meeting	• Appropriately engaging in group activities • Asking questions or sharing ideas that relate to the activity • Listening to ideas and comments from peers • Paying attention to a lesson and ignoring distractions from peers who are off-task or other adults coming into the room • Raising a hand, taking turns, and allowing peers to have a turn • Transitioning to and from group time following instructions
	Music and movement	• Following instructions • Starting and stopping singing, dancing, or playing instruments in response to teacher cues
	Outdoor time	• Following classroom safety rules (e.g., using walking feet when reentering the building, one child at a time on the slide) • Regulating emotions (excitement, sadness, frustration) effectively during independent play and when playing with peers • Waiting for a turn on playground equipment and allowing peers to have a turn

Group Size	Activity	Ways that Children Might Demonstrate Self-Regulation
Small group	Read alouds/ shared reading	• Actively listening and actively participating at times when it is appropriate to do so • Asking questions that show attention to the story • Ignoring interruptions or distractions • Responding to questions from teachers or peers
	Transitions	• Putting an activity away in response to the cleanup song • Switching attention from one activity to another activity
	Learning centers	• Waiting for a turn to use art supplies (e.g., scissors or a glue stick) rather than taking them from a classmate • Following classroom rules related to learning centers (e.g., only four children allowed at the science table at one time)
	Snack or meal times	• Engaging in conversations with teachers and peers • Asking for help when needed • Helping set up the snack/lunch table • Passing food to a classmate • Waiting to eat until the appropriate time and taking turns serving food
	Waiting (e.g., standing in line to use the bathroom)	• Engaging in appropriate activities while waiting (e.g., singing a song, talking with a teacher or friend) • Showing awareness of self and peers (e.g., standing or sitting an appropriate distance from others without pushing) • Waiting for others to finish before taking a turn
Individual	Individual/ free play	• Asking for help when needed • Choosing appropriate tasks to engage in (e.g., art activities, blocks, puzzles) • Following through and finishing a task that has been started • Putting one activity away before starting another activity
	Drop-off and pickup	• Asking for help from a teacher to find an activity • Finding a teacher or friend for comfort if feeling sad saying good-bye • Putting personal items into a cubby (e.g., hanging up a coat or backpack) • Saying good-bye and separating from parents/caregivers

● ● ● ● ●

Self-Regulation: "Cool" and "Hot"

The list in Table 1.2 gives examples of many times throughout the day when children are asked to pay attention to a lesson or a task, start and stop an activity, switch attention from one activity to another, wait for a turn, or control an impulse. Demonstrating self-regulation can be challenging for children (and adults too!). During the early childhood years, children are at many different stages in their development of these skills, so they need practice! At the end of each chapter, we provide activities for you to try in your classroom to help children practice and develop these skills. Practicing paying attention, remembering instructions, and controlling impulses through fun and engaging games is one way to help children strengthen their self-regulation abilities so that they can function effectively throughout the day. There is another important component of self-regulation that needs to be considered that we have not yet discussed.

What's missing so far from our discussion is the context (both physical and emotional) in which children are asked to self-regulate. For example, paying attention at circle time may be easy for a child, Leia, on a day when she is well-rested and fed, her teacher has chosen her favorite book, and Jonny (a child who struggles with self-regulation and often tantrums during circle time) is absent. Would self-regulation still be easy for Leia if all of these factors were not in place? What if Leia had a rough morning at home, struggled with saying good-bye to her mom, and came to school feeling sad? What if her teacher was feeling overwhelmed and did not have time to plan circle time the way she usually did and found herself reading a book that was not engaging and too long? What if Jonny was present and having a bad day and his tantrums were distracting and upsetting to Leia? The context surrounding a child affects not only a child's development of self-regulation (discussed in greater detail in Chapter 2) but also a child's ability to self-regulate in the moment. What is happening in a child's life at home and at school contributes to a child's emotional state. Research shows that emotions have a profound impact on self-regulation (e.g., attention and memory) as well as learning (Brackett, Rivers, Maurer, Elbertson, & Kremenitzer, 2011). Have you ever attended a class or a meeting while you were feeling stressed or overwhelmed? How well did you pay attention? How much did you remember? Think about how having these feelings might impact a child's ability to pay attention at circle time and interact positively with peers and teachers.

When we defined self-regulation at the beginning of the chapter, our definition included the regulation of thoughts, behaviors, and emotions. Up to this point, our examples have primarily focused on regulating thoughts and behaviors—"cool" aspects of regulation. "Cool" aspects of regulation are elicited when children (or adults) are asked to perform abstract tasks, like sorting colors or numbers. "Hot" aspects of regulation are elicited when children or adults are asked to complete tasks that tap into emotion and motivation, like participating in a frustrating task or delaying gratification

(Hongwanishkul, Happaney, Lee, & Zelazo, 2005). Let's consider the following example:

Jessy loved to play Simon Says. He would watch his teacher attentively, copying each of her actions by touching his head, touching his nose, waving his arms—but only when she said, "Simon says." He was an expert at the "Freeze Game" and would dance energetically while the music played and freeze instantly when the music stopped. In games like these, Jessy's self-regulatory abilities were strong. There were other times, however, when Jessy had trouble self-regulating. For example, when Jessy became frustrated trying to tie his shoe himself, his teacher asked if he needed help and Jessy responded by throwing his shoe. When Jessy became angry after another child took his glue stick, he immediately pushed the child to the floor and grabbed the glue stick back. His teacher, Ms. Nancy, noticed that Jessy's difficulties with self-regulation most often occurred when he was emotionally triggered and that it was during those times that Jessy's ability to think before acting seemed to vanish. She continued playing self-regulation games with Jessy and the rest of her class to help them practice these skills, but worried that these games might not be enough to help Jessy learn to regulate during emotionally charged moments.

In this example, Jessy's struggle with self-regulation occurred most frequently when he was called on to use "hot" aspects of regulation. Unlike the situations in this example, however, many situations that require self-regulation do not fall neatly into the "hot" or the "cool" category. Thus, it is important for early childhood educators to develop a toolbox of strategies to support children's ability to successfully self-regulate in situations that require either "hot" or "cool" strategies or both!

● ● ● ● ●

The Relationship Between Emotions and Behavior

Jessy's challenges with self-regulation in emotionally charged situations are not uncommon. The brain's natural reaction to emotionally charged situations is familiarly called a "fight or flight response." In response to stress or intense emotions, the brain produces cortisol—a hormone that helps us react quickly in response to danger, but one that also inhibits pathways to the prefrontal cortex (the area of the brain associated with self-regulation) (Hanson et al., 2012). In other words, when a strong emotional response is triggered, we will likely have trouble making good decisions like Jessy. Our ability to stop and think before acting can be impaired. Learning to recognize when this is happening in children (and ourselves) can help us support children with strategies for calming down when they are upset so that they can effectively regulate their emotions, thoughts, and behaviors.

●●●●●

Learning Checkpoint

1. Think about the relationship between emotions and behaviors. How does understanding how a child is feeling affect the way you might respond to his or her behaviors? How might you respond to each of the following examples? How would your response differ based on a child's feeling?

    a. A child is having difficulty paying attention at circle time because she is feeling sad and misses her mom.

    b. A child is having difficulty paying attention at circle time because she is feeling excited about an upcoming field trip.

    c. A child is having difficulty paying attention at circle time because she is frustrated that she did not have enough time to finish her painting at the easel.

    d. A child is having difficulty paying attention at circle time because she is feeling bored.

2. Brainstorm a list of triggers that occur throughout the day at school and at home that might cause unpleasant or intense emotions (e.g., anger, frustration, stress) for children in your class. Do the same triggers affect different children in the same way or different ways?

3. Brainstorm a list of triggers that occur throughout the day that might cause you to experience unpleasant or intense emotions. How often do these triggers arise and how do they affect your ability to teach or interact with others? How do you manage your own feelings of stress in the moment (e.g., taking deep breaths) and in the long term (e.g., exercising, seeking support from others)?

In the final section of this chapter, we provide tips for helping children regulate intense emotions and calm down when emotionally triggered. We conclude by encouraging you to reflect on what you have learned in this chapter and to set a goal relevant to your work as an early childhood professional.

●●●●●

Tips for Helping Children Learn to Regulate Intense Emotions

1. *Start by helping children learn what "calm" feels like.* Children often hear the phrase "calm down," but what does "calm" mean to a child? Provide children with opportunities that help them experience the feeling calm so that they have an understanding of how their body

feels at times when they feel calm, can think clearly, and regulate effectively.

a. Practice deep breathing. During small or large group time, practice taking deep breaths together. Have children lie on their backs with a stuffed animal on their stomach and watch as it rises and falls. If stuffed animals are not available, pretend to smell a flower when breathing in and blow bubbles or blow out birthday candles when breathing out.

b. Engage children in stretching and yoga. Stretch together by reaching up toward the sky to pick apples or down to the ground to make a snowball. Use pictures of adults, children, or animals in various yoga poses to demonstrate to children what to do or model yoga poses yourself and ask children to imitate you. Count together from 1 to 10 (or 20) or backward from 10 to 1 as you hold each pose.

c. Give children opportunities to practice controlling their bodies through slow dancing and movement. Dance around with streamers to slow classical music. Have children transition from one activity (e.g., leaving group time to choose a learning center; walking down the hall on the way outside) to another by moving as slowly as a turtle or a snail. A list of recommended songs for helping children experience calm feelings is provided in Chapter 9.

d. Help children learn to notice changes in their body during calm and high-energy activities. Ask children to place their hands on their chests to feel their hearts beating after jumping up and down or dancing to fast music. After participating in one or more of the calm activities presented earlier, ask children to feel their hearts again and notice the difference—when calm, it is much harder to feel your heart beating in your chest and it beats much more slowly.

2. *Teach children how to recognize what a range of emotions look and feel like.* Read books, share stories, and use role-plays focused on characters that experience different emotions, particularly those that children in your classroom might struggle with (e.g., anger, frustration, disappointment). A list of book recommendations is provided in Chapter 9.

a. Ask children questions that help them recognize what different emotions look and feel like (in the characters as well as in themselves), understand different things that happen that cause these feelings, and things we can do when we have these feelings to show them appropriately and regulate them. Teaching children about regulating their emotions in this way outside of emotionally charged situations lays a foundation that will enable children to apply these skills in emotionally charged moments.

b. Create a glitter jar. Fill a plastic water bottle with water and glitter (add glycerin to keep the glitter from sticking to itself). Use the jar as a prop to show children how their brain becomes clouded, making it hard to think, when they are upset. Take deep breaths together as the glitter settles to help children think about the importance of feeling calm before acting.

3. *Take time to acknowledge and validate children's feelings.* Helping children recognize the feelings they are having is an important step to helping them learn to manage these feelings appropriately.

   a. Label children's feelings when they are experiencing unpleasant or intense emotions like frustration, anger, disappointment, or sadness, and let them know that these feelings are okay ("It looks like you are feeling frustrated. I feel frustrated too when I have trouble doing something by myself.").

   b. Allow children time to express their unpleasant emotions, and help them do so in a way that is appropriate in your classroom. For example, hitting another child out of frustration is not an appropriate way to express anger in any classroom, but saying, "I'm *mad!*" and hitting or squeezing a pillow in the quiet corner might be. Children need to be taught and given opportunities to practice strategies that will take the place of their impulses. These strategies for demonstrating emotions appropriately need to be modeled and practiced outside of emotionally charged situations first so that children will be better equipped to turn to them in emotionally charged moments.

Reflect

After reading this chapter, think about the strategies, games, and activities you currently use in your classroom to help children practice self-regulation. If you are not currently teaching in a classroom, make a list of games that you know or games you played as a child that focus on self-regulation.

■ When and how often do you use these activities in your class?
■ How do children typically respond to these types of activities?

Set a Goal

Identify a specific self-regulation skill (e.g., paying attention, calming down after experiencing an intense emotion, exhibiting inhibitory control). What is one way you could help children practice this specific skill more often?

● ● ● ● ●

Additional Resources

See Chapter 9 for additional resources related to the contents of this chapter, including Internet resources; children's books on feelings, managing emotions, and calming strategies; and songs to help children experience feeling calm.

● ● ● ● ●

References

Blair, C., & Diamond, A. (2008). Biological processes in prevention and intervention: The promotion of self-regulation as a means of preventing school failure. *Development and Psychopathology, 20*(3), 899–911. doi:10.1017/S0954579408000436

Brackett, M., Rivers, S., Maurer, M., Elbertson, N., & Kremenitzer, J. (2011). *Creating emotionally literate classrooms: An introduction to The RULER Approach to social and emotional learning.* Port Chester, NY: National Professional Resources.

Denham, S. A., & Weissberg, R. P. (2004). Social-emotional learning in early childhood. In E. Chesebrough, P. King, T. P. Gullotta, & M. Bloom (Eds.), *A blueprint for the promotion of prosocial behavior in early childhood* (pp. 13–50). New York, NY: Kluwer Academic/Plenum.

Diamond, A. (2010). The evidence base for improving school outcomes by addressing the whole child and by addressing skills and attitudes, not just content. *Early Education & Development, 21*(5), 780–793. doi:10.1080/10409289.2010.514522

Dowsett, S. M., & Livesey, D. J. (2000). The development of inhibitory control in preschool children: Effects of "executive skills" training. *Developmental Psychobiology, 36*(2), 161–174.

Eisenberg, N., Eggum, N. D., Sallquist, J., & Edwards, A. (2010). Relations of self-regulatory/control capacities to maladjustment, social competence, and emotionality. In R. H. Hoyle (Ed.), *Handbook of personality and self-regulation* (pp. 19–46). Oxford: Wiley-Blackwell.

Garon, N., Bryson, S. E., & Smith, I. M. (2008). Executive function in preschoolers: A review using an integrative framework. *Psychological Bulletin, 134*(1), 31–60. doi:10.1037/0033-2909.134.1.31

Gathercole, S. E. (2008). Working memory in the classroom. *Psychologist, 21*(5), 382–385.

Gilliam, W. S., & Shabar, G. (2006). Preschool and child care expulsion and suspension: Rates and predictors in one state. *Infants & Young Children: An Interdisciplinary Journal of Special Care Practices, 19*(3), 228–245.

Hanson, J. L., Chung, M. K., Avants, B. B., Rudolph, K. D., Shirtcliff, E. A., Gee, J. C., . . . Pollak, S. D. (2012). Structural variations in prefrontal cortex mediate the relationship between early childhood stress and spatial working memory. *Journal of Neuroscience, 32*(23), 7917–7925.

Hongwanishkul, D., Happaney, K. R., Lee, W.S.C., & Zelazo, P. D. (2005). Assessment of hot and cool executive function in young children: Age-related changes and individual differences. *Developmental Neuropsychology, 28*(2), 617–644.

Ladd, G.W., Birch, S.H., & Buhs, E.S. (1999). Children's social and scholastic lives in kindergarten: Related spheres of influence? *Child Development, 70,* 1373–1400.

Ladd, G.W., & Dinella, L.M. (2009). Continuity and change in early school engagement: Predictive of children's achievement trajectories from first to eighth grade? *Journal of Educational Psychology, 101*(1), 190–206. doi:10.1037/a0013153

McClelland, M.M., & Cameron, C.E. (2011). Self-regulation and academic achievement in elementary school children. *New Directions for Child and Adolescent Development, 2011*(133), 29–44. doi:10.1002/cd.302

McClelland, M.M., Ponitz, C.C., Messersmith, E.E., & Tominey, S. (2010). Self-regulation: The integration of cognition and emotion. In R. Lerner (Series Ed.) & W. Overton (Vol. Ed.), *Handbook of lifespan human development: Vol. 1. Cognition, biology and methods* (pp. 509–553). Hoboken, NJ: Wiley.

Rimm-Kaufman, S.E., Pianta, R.C., & Cox, M.J. (2000). Teachers' judgments of problems in the transition to kindergarten. *Early Childhood Research Quarterly, 15*(2), 147–166.

Rueda, M.R., Posner, M.I., & Rothbart, M.K. (2005). The development of executive attention: contributions to the emergence of self-regulation. *Developmental Neuropsychology, 28*(2), 573–594.

Tominey, S.L., & Rivers, S.E. (2012). *Social-emotional skills in preschool education in the state of Connecticut: Current practice and implications for child development.* Report prepared for the William Casper Graustein Memorial Fund.

Zsolnai, A. (2002). Relationship between children's social competence, learning motivation and school achievement. *Educational Psychology, 22*(3), 317–329.

2

●●●●●

Laying the Foundation for Self-Regulation

The car starts and three-month-old Carina begins to cry. Her mother's voice from the front seat ("I'm here, Carina.") soothes her momentarily, but then she starts to cry again. As the car moves forward, Carina finds her fist and calms down as she begins to suck on it.

Darius holds his dad's hand as he walks into the doctor's office for his two-year checkup. He sits on his dad's lap and watches his dad's face for a reaction as the doctor walks into the room. His dad shakes Dr. Martinez's hand, and Darius gives her a high five.

Addy sits next to her friend Mo at circle time. Mo keeps playing with the tag on Addy's sweater rather than paying attention to the book their teacher is reading. Addy tells Mo, "Please stop," and then ignores Mo's actions and focuses her attention on Ms. Jackie so that she does not miss the story.

Although each of these scenarios presents children in different contexts and different stages of development, each provides an example of how self-regulation might look in early childhood. Most children experience significant growth in self-regulation during preschool, but self-regulation development begins long before children set foot in a preschool classroom. In fact, self-regulation is beginning to emerge even from birth! In this chapter, we provide an overview of how self-regulation develops, with a focus on what early childhood educators can do to lay a foundation for the development of these skills. We conclude by sharing specific tips for ways that educators can promote self-regulation through building secure and trusting relationships with children, modeling strong self-regulation skills, and adopting caregiving and teaching practices that promote critical thinking and perspective taking.

● ● ● ● ●

Self-Regulation Development: From External to Internal Regulation

As we mentioned at the beginning of this chapter, self-regulation development is already beginning at birth. In infancy, self-regulation is primarily an external process (McClelland, Ponitz, Messersmith, & Tominey, 2010). What this means is that other people (parents and caregivers) most often provide regulation for a child. Children typically provide cues when they need help regulating (e.g., by crying or cooing) and look to an adult (parent or caregiver) to help regulate their needs. For example, when a baby cries, a responsive parent or caregiver will help calm a baby by holding, rocking, soothing, changing the baby's diaper, or feeding the baby. As children grow and develop, self-regulation shifts from an external process to an increasingly internal process. For example, instead of relying on her mom to calm her down in the foregoing example, Carina soothed herself by sucking on her fist. Darius regulated his nervousness at the doctor's office by using cues from his father's reaction to determine that this was a safe environment. Addy regulated her attention herself by using language to ask Mo to stop, consciously ignoring him when he continued playing with her tag, and keeping her focus on Ms. Jackie. The shift from external to internal regulation is a slow and gradual one—one that happens over time and in stages. Although Carina was able to effectively soothe herself on this car ride, she might not be able to do the same thing next time, but it will happen more and more frequently as she practices, grows, and develops.

Numerous factors play a role in a child's ability to make the shift from external to internal regulation, including:

■ The attachment relationship between children and caregivers (educators and family members);
■ A child's exposure to adults and peers who model strong self-regulation skills;
■ The caregiving styles of key adults in a child's life;
■ A child's maturation and brain development related to self-regulation;
■ The opportunities a child has to learn and practice self-regulation (Bernier, Carlson, & Whipple, 2010; McClelland et al., 2010).

Table 2.1 provides an overview of how self-regulation develops across early childhood along with examples of how self-regulation might look at various developmental stages.

Table 2.1 Developmental Milestones of Self-Regulation

Age range	Developmental progression	How this might look
Early infancy (0–6 months)	Temperament plays an important role in how children react to new experiences and how easily they calm down. Self-regulation is primarily external. Early signs of self-regulation begin to emerge.	• Crying or cooing to express needs • Focusing on faces and interesting patterns • Self-soothing (e.g., sucking on a fist) • Turning head away from unwanted sounds or people
Late infancy (6 months–24 months)	Self-regulation is still largely externally regulated by adults. Children start to demonstrate working memory, maintain attention for short periods of time, and show early signs of controlling emotions and behavior.	• Calming down in response to adult cues and responses • Persisting on engaging tasks for a short time • Remembering salient locations when driving in a car • Searching for hidden objects • Showing recognition of key people in their lives (e.g., family members and caregivers)
Toddlerhood (24–36 months; 2–3 years)	Self-regulation starts to move from external to internal control as children learn to comply and internalize adult commands and requests.	• Using cues from parents/caregivers to decide how to respond to new people or situations • Using private speech to say things like "Don't touch the stove—it's hot!"
Preschool (3–5 years)	Rapid development in self-regulation parallels rapid growth in brain development. Children start to develop theory of mind or an understanding that others have thoughts and feelings that may differ from their own. Perspective-taking abilities begin to develop, but children are still largely egocentric and may have difficulty seeing other perspectives.	• Demonstrating self-regulation during make-believe play with others • Remembering and following multi-step instructions, and demonstrating self-control of emotions and behavior • Showing persistence on activities like puzzles and blocks • Using private speech as a regulation strategy
Kindergarten (5–6 years)	Rapid growth in brain development continues and is accompanied by development in self-regulation. Children's theory of mind continues to develop, and children become less egocentric and increase their perspective-taking skills. Metacognition increases and can be used to reflect on children's own thinking. Children start to use self-regulation strategies and do so more consistently.	• Cooperating and playing well with peers • Demonstrating a range of strategies to regulate behaviors, emotions, and thoughts • Increasing ability to persist on and complete tasks • Remembering, following, and completing multi-step instructions

● ● ● ● ●

Laying a Foundation for Self-Regulation: The Caregiver-Child Attachment Relationship

The development of a secure and trusting relationship (or a secure attachment) between a child and at least one caregiver lays the foundation for numerous positive outcomes, including self-regulation (Calkins, 2004). A secure attachment is formed when a caregiver provides consistent sensitive and responsive care, adapting his or her caregiving to fit the individual needs of the child (Bowlby, 1988). Although most infants have many of the same needs (food, diapering, comfort, sleep, love, and attention), the cues they show through facial expressions, body language, crying, and cooing may be drastically different. Some children rarely cry and soothe quickly. Other children are highly reactive, cry easily, and take significant effort to calm down. Most children fall somewhere in between these extremes. How reactive children are and how easily they calm down relate to their temperament—the individual differences that serve as the foundation for a child's personality (Eisenberg, Vaughan, & Hofer, 2009). Children are born with different styles and temperaments, and these individual differences play out in the classroom in many ways. It is also important to note that children's temperament is malleable, however, and can be influenced by caregivers and the environment, especially early in a child's life.

Regardless of whether we are aware of it, a child's temperament and personality can affect the way that educators approach and react to a child. Studies have shown that children with more highly reactive temperaments are rated lower by teachers on a "teachability" scale (Keogh, 2013). In other words, teachers find it more challenging to teach children who react strongly in emotional situations and who take more effort to calm down than their peers. Other studies have shown that teachers spend more time with children who have easy temperaments (Keogh, 1986). This is not surprising, but what is concerning is the fact that studies also show that educators may not be aware of inequities that exist in the way they view and treat students (Keogh, 2013). Studies like these have important implications for early childhood educators. The match between a child and an adult (educator or parent/caregiver) can be thought of in terms of a "goodness of fit" (Rothbart, Posner, & Kieras, 2006). Goodness of fit refers to the compatibility between a child's temperament and his or her environment, including their learning environments (Thomas & Chess, 1986). Educators who foster goodness of fit in their relationships with children adjust their teaching approach to match the temperament of each individual child (Keogh, 1986), laying a foundation that supports early learning.

Think about the children you have known or worked with—no two children are alike. As adults, we often find that our personalities are a better match with some people than with others. This is also true for the relationships we have with children in our classrooms. As educators, we want to be able to support children's growth and development no matter how easy or difficult it is for us to connect with each child, but the truth is that this can be a challenge. Recognizing the fact that we may naturally connect with some children more easily than others is an important step toward recognizing how the connections we have (or struggle to have) can affect our ability to effectively teach a child and may affect a child's ability to effectively learn from us.

● ● ● ● ●

Learning Checkpoint

1. Think about the children in your life—the children in your personal life or family or the children in your classroom.
   a. Have there been children whom you have connected with easily and naturally? Are there characteristics that these children have in common?
   b. Have there been children with whom you have struggled to build a connection or whose actions and words have triggered a response in you? What characteristics (in the child or yourself) have made those connections a struggle?
   c. How do you think being aware of these characteristics might help you better connect with children in the future?

Developing a secure relationship with children can be a challenge for many reasons. These challenges are evident in the fact that only 60%–65% of infants have a secure attachment with a parental figure (Berk, 2012), indicating that 35%–40% of infants do not. Children whose parents are unavailable, disengaged, or chronically inattentive are more likely to have insecure attachments and to experience difficulty with close relationships later in life (Bowlby, 1988; Calkins, 2004; Sroufe, 1997). Families in high-risk settings may experience numerous factors (e.g., chronic poverty, family turmoil, economic and employment instability) that contribute to psychological stress and that impact parenting abilities (Evans & Kim, 2013), challenging the ability of parents to effectively establish secure relationships with children.

Although there is some debate as to whether the teacher-child relationship meets the definition of an attachment relationship, there is plenty of evidence that children can build warm and trusting relationships with their teachers and that these relationships play an important role in helping children develop self-regulation and other skills necessary for building positive relationships and engaging in learning (Commodari, 2013; Denham, Bassett, & Zinsser, 2012; Drake, Belsky, & Fearon, 2014; Howes, 2000; Rothbart et al., 2006). Studies have found that children who are more engaged with their teachers make greater gains in self-regulation in comparison to their peers with lower engagement (Williford, Vick Whittaker, Vitiello, & Downer, 2013). The risks associated with insecure attachments suggest that it may be especially important for early childhood educators to develop a secure attachment (sometimes called an "earned attachment") with children who may not otherwise have a secure relationship with a parental or family figure.

Why Building Secure and Trusting Relationships Matters for Self-Regulation

Educators who establish secure attachment relationships and a goodness of fit send a message to children that they can be trusted and relied on. This relationship also helps children feel secure and safe. By 2–3 years, children have developed an internal set of expectations for the important people in their lives (Ainsworth, Blehar, Waters, & Wall, 1988; Bowlby, 1988). If children have learned that these important people will respond with warmth and support when they ask for attention and help, they are more likely to seek comfort from adults, look to adults as models of behavior, and look forward to engaging in learning activities with adults. The shift of self-regulation from an internal to an external process relies on this foundation provided by the development of secure and supportive relationships.

●●●●●

Laying a Foundation for Self-Regulation: Modeling Self-Regulation

Intentionally modeling strong self-regulation abilities is also an important part of promoting children's self-regulation development. Educators who effectively model strong self-regulation skills across the day provide children with a framework of what "to do" rather than what "not to do." Having models is critical for a child's ability to demonstrate self-regulation while navigating social and academic situations. Developing awareness of their own self-regulation abilities is also beneficial to educators. Self-regulation helps adults effectively manage their own thoughts, feelings, and behaviors, especially when they are upset. Research suggests that caregivers who have strong self-regulation abilities are more likely to demonstrate nurturing and responsive caregiving, interact more effectively with their children, and are more likely to promote these skills in young children (Sanders & Mazzucchelli, 2013).

Mr. Acock smiles and greets each child and family as they come through the classroom door each morning. He reminds children to wash their hands first before choosing an activity and makes sure that he washes his own hands several times throughout the morning so that children see him doing so. One morning, he realizes that he has not yet washed his own hands. He stands in line at the sink behind another child, commenting, "I forgot to wash my hands! I will wait right here to have a turn when you are finished."

Through modeling, Mr. Acock is using actions and words to demonstrate the rules and routines of the classroom. By sharing his private speech out loud, he is modeling his thought process for children, letting them know it is okay to make a mistake and demonstrating evidence of his own self-regulation abilities.

Consider some of the opportunities that educators have to demonstrate self-regulation across the span of a day at school (opportunities for parents to model self-regulation are discussed in Chapter 7). During the preschool day, educators can model self-regulation in many different ways, including by:

■ Staying engaged with children throughout the day and ignoring distractions (e.g., the temptation to daydream or check text messages);

■ Modeling waiting for a turn (e.g., waiting to wash hands until after a child has finished);

■ Allowing children to take their time and do something on their own (e.g., put on a coat or cut a shape with scissors by themselves), rather than completing a task for a child because it would be faster;

■ Responding calmly and appropriately to triggers that arise throughout the day (e.g., interruptions during circle time from children or other adults, children's temper tantrums).

● ● ● ● ●

Learning Checkpoint

1. Can you think of times during the day when you can model self-regulation for children in your role as an educator? Make a list of as many opportunities as you can think of in which you (or other

educators) can model self-regulation for children throughout the day. Be as specific as possible.

a. Put a check next to each item on your list that you feel you already model well for the children in your classroom.

b. Circle each entry on your list that you feel you could model more often for children in your classroom.

c. What is one thing you can do to model self-regulation more often?

●●●●●

Laying a Foundation for Self-Regulation: Using an Authoritative Caregiving Style

In addition to modeling self-regulation abilities throughout the day, educators can adopt teaching and caregiving styles that promote self-regulation. An authoritative caregiving style, one characterized by positive control, autonomy support, and responsiveness, is linked most often to strong self-regulation (Bernier et al., 2010; Karreman, van Tuijl, van Aken, & Deković, 2006). An important characteristic of authoritative caregiving is a focus on communication and the use of language (Bindman, Hindman, Bowles, & Morrison, 2013). For example, educators using an authoritative style may communicate expectations to children prior to a transition or activity to let children know what they should expect, what is expected of them, and why. They are also more likely to explain to children the reasoning behind disciplinary actions in a way that is developmentally appropriate for children. Rather than using ultimatums—such as "Because I said so!"—an educator using an authoritative style might say, "I am taking the scissors away from you because what you were doing was not safe, and I do not want you to get hurt or to hurt someone else. We can try again later using the scissors while you are sitting at the table." Hearing, "Because I said so," teaches a child not to do something temporarily, but the child doesn't understand *why*. Hearing and understanding the reason *why* not to do certain things help children internalize the message and develop critical thinking skills necessary to eventually regulate their own behaviors.

The language that educators and caregivers use with children during early childhood comes at an important time. Children make tremendous gains in language during the early childhood years (Goldin-Meadow, 2006), and these gains help them understand and interact with the world around them. If the language a child hears is rich with descriptive words and vocabulary that describe actions as well as the reasons behind these actions, children's own thoughts begin to follow these patterns.

Consider Hannah and her teacher, Ms. Linda, in the following scenario.

Hannah is four. She is sitting at a table with several of her classmates and her teacher, Ms. Linda. They are building sculptures with play-dough. Hannah reaches over and takes a ball of play-dough from Julien, who is sitting next to her. Julien immediately pouts. Ms. Linda says, "Hannah, I saw you take that from Julien. Give it back." Hannah shakes her head, but Ms. Linda insists. "Give it back now. I told you to stop doing that. You're done at this table. Go find something else to do."

In this example, Ms. Linda uses language to tell Hannah what not to do. Rather than providing Hannah with an alternative approach to finding more play-dough, Ms. Linda removed Hannah from the situation. Unfortunately, this resulted in a missed opportunity to help Hannah practice self-regulation skills, perspective taking, and problem solving. This might have been the second time Hannah had taken play-dough from another child or the tenth. Without guidance helping her think about what she can do when she wants more play-dough, Hannah will likely return to the table and try the same thing again, especially when Ms. Linda is not looking.

Now consider the same scenario, but with Ms. Linda taking a different approach.

Hannah reaches over and takes a ball of play-dough from Julien, who is sitting next to her. Julien immediately pouts. Ms. Linda says, "Hannah, it looks like you need more play-dough for your sculpture. Are you feeling frustrated that you cannot have more? How do you think Julien felt when you took it from him?" Hannah looks at Julien's face and says, "Sad." Ms. Linda asks Hannah what she could do to help Julien feel better. Hannah hands the play-dough back to Julien, and Julien smiles as he starts to play again. Ms. Linda continues: "I wonder what you could do if you need more play-dough and feel frustrated. Do you have any ideas?" Hannah shakes her head. Ms. Linda says, "Let's look around the table and see if we can find some play-dough that no one else is using. Do you see any?" Again, Hannah shakes her head. Ms. Linda suggests, "Maybe you could ask Julien if you can use his play-dough when he is finished." Hannah does, and Julien hands her his pile of play-dough when he leaves to paint at the easel.

In the second example, Ms. Linda uses language that helps Hannah put words to her actions, consider the reasons for her actions, consider the consequences of those actions and Julien's feelings (perspective taking), and follow through with a pro-social solution (problem solving). Linda is laying an important foundation that will help Hannah navigate this situation or situations like it by herself in the future. This does not mean that the next time Hannah sits at the play-dough table, she will remember to look for play-dough that no one else is playing with or ask first, but it does increase the chance that Hannah will begin thinking through these steps on her own. The more times Hannah is supported through scenarios like this one, the more likely she will be to internally self-regulate in the future. It is important to note that helping children walk through a situation in this way takes time. It takes several minutes, and that is significantly longer than the seconds it takes to send a child away from an activity with no explanation, but the long-term benefit is tremendous.

● ● ● ● ●

Brain Development and Maturation Related to Self-Regulation

Creating an environment that effectively supports children's self-regulation development during early childhood through building secure relationships, modeling, and using an authoritative caregiving style is important because this is a key developmental period of growth for self-regulation. For most children, preschool is the first classroom environment that they experience and thus their first opportunity to demonstrate and practice self-regulation with teachers and peers (Denton Flanagan & McPhee, 2009; Phillips, McCartney, & Sussman, 2006). Early childhood is also when children experience significant growth in the prefrontal cortex, the area of the brain related to self-regulation (Blair, 2002). This brain development supports children's ability to internally regulate as well as the development of a number of related skills, including theory of mind (the understanding that others have thoughts and feelings too), which supports children's critical thinking and perspective-taking abilities (Schneider, Schumann-Hengsteler, & Sodian, 2005).

Together, these factors point to preschool as a critical period for self-regulation development and intervention. Intentionally promoting self-regulation skills during preschool has the potential to maximize children's self-regulation growth at a critical period of development, ensuring that children have the skills they need for success in preschool, across the transition to kindergarten, and throughout their schooling.

In the final section of this chapter, we provide tips for laying a foundation for self-regulation development in early childhood through building secure and trusting relationships with children, modeling self-regulation, and using an authoritative caregiving style.

● ● ● ● ●

Tips for Laying a Foundation for Self-Regulation Development

1. *Build secure and trusting relationships with children in your classroom.*

   a. Be present and actively engaged with children throughout the day. Practice strategies (e.g., reminding yourself of the importance of engaging with children, taking pleasure in children's joys) that help you ignore the temptation to daydream or check text messages so that you can be present with the children in your classroom.

   b. Foster a strong goodness of fit by getting to know children as individuals and learning their temperamental style. Take time while sitting with children around the snack or lunch table, while helping children wait in line, or during individual play to have conversations with children about their likes and dislikes, their families, and other things important to them.

   c. Help children get to know you by sharing personal stories about yourself that are developmentally appropriate for children. Tell children about your likes and dislikes, your family, and the feelings that you have throughout the day. Getting to know you helps children feel safe and secure in your care.

2. *Model strong self-regulation skills.*

   a. Identify opportunities in your day to model self-regulation. Think through a typical day for yourself, and identify two or three opportunities that you have to model self-regulation for the children in your classroom. Set a goal to intentionally model for children during these times. When modeling self-regulation, say your private speech out loud to explain to children what you are doing and why ("I feel really hungry for lunch, but I know I need to wash my hands first, just like you.").

   b. Model regulation of your own unpleasant emotions and stress. A study examining the effectiveness of a school readiness intervention in preschool found that receiving professional development related to stress reduction for teachers was associated with improvements in self-regulation and early academic skills for children in their classrooms (Raver et al., 2011).

   c. Practice, practice, practice, and realize that developing and modeling self-regulation are a process, especially in emotionally charged situations (e.g., responding to a child with severe behavioral difficulties). Building strong self-regulation is a process for both children and adults and takes time. Allow yourself room for error in practicing these skills, and allow room for children to make mistakes as they practice and develop their own skills.

3. *Use an authoritative teaching style.*

   a. Talk, talk, talk. Talk about everything you do with the children in your class, and explain the reasons behind the choices you make. Describing what you see as objectively as possible contributes to fostering a secure and trusting relationship and helps children learn about you and how you think. It also helps children understand the world around them, and build perspective-taking abilities and critical thinking skills—all of which are related to strong self-regulation.

   b. Prepare children for transitions. Before each transition that occurs throughout the day, take time to explain to children what is coming next so that they know what to expect as well as what is expected of them. Helping children feel prepared for what is coming next provides them with information that will help them more easily regulate their response to the situation.

   c. Provide children with opportunities to practice self-regulation skills throughout the day. The songs, activities, and games presented in the "Activity Breaks" throughout this book provide specific ideas for how self-regulation can be practiced and improved.

Reflect

What is one thing you do that helps you build secure relationships with the children in your classroom? What is one way that you help foster secure relationships between the children in your classroom?

Set a Goal

Identify two specific strategies presented in this chapter that you would like to do more of in your current teaching practice or in your interactions with children. What are they and what will you do to integrate these strategies into your approach?

● ● ● ● ●

Additional Resources

See Chapter 9 for additional resources related to the contents of this chapter, including Internet resources focusing on supporting self-regulation development.

• • • • •

References

Ainsworth, M.D.S., Blehar, M. C., Waters, E., & Wall, S. (1978). *Patterns of attachment: A psychological study of the strange situation*. Hillsdale, NJ: Erlbaum.

Berk, L. E. (2012). *Infants and children: Prenatal through middle childhood* (7th ed.). Boston, MA: Allyn & Bacon.

Bernier, A., Carlson, S. M., & Whipple, N. (2010). From external regulation to self-regulation: Early parenting precursors of young children's executive functioning. *Child Development, 81*(1), 326–339.

Bindman, S.W., Hindman, A. H., Bowles, R. P., & Morrison, F. J. (2013). The contributions of parental management language to executive function in preschool children. *Early Childhood Research Quarterly, 28*(3), 529–539.

Blair, C. (2002). School readiness. *American Psychologist, 57*(2), 111.

Bowlby, J. (1988). *A secure base: Parent-child attachment and healthy human development*. London: Routledge.

Calkins, S. D. (2004). Early attachment processes and the development of emotional self-regulation. In R. F. Baumeister & K. D. Vohs (Eds.), *Handbook of self-regulation: Research, theory, and applications* (pp. 324–339). New York, NY: Guilford Press.

Commodari, E. (2013). Preschool teacher attachment, school readiness and risk of learning difficulties. *Early Childhood Research Quarterly, 28*(1), 123–133. doi:10.1016/j.ecresq.2012.03.004

Denham, S. A., Bassett, H. H., & Zinsser, K. (2012). Early childhood teachers as socializers of young children's emotional competence. *Early Childhood Education Journal, 40*(3), 137–143.

Denton Flanagan, K., & McPhee, C. (2009). *The children born in 2001 at kindergarten entry: First findings from the kindergarten data collections of the Early Childhood Longitudinal Study, Birth Cohort (ECLS-B)* (NCES 2010–005). Washington, DC: National Center for Education Statistics, Institute of Education Sciences, U.S. Department of Education.

Drake, K., Belsky, J., & Fearon, R.M.P. (2014). From early attachment to engagement with learning in school: The role of self-regulation and persistence. *Developmental Psychology, 50*(5), 1350–1361. doi:10.1037/a0032779

Eisenberg, N., Vaughan, J., & Hofer, C. (2009). Temperament, self-regulation, and peer social competence. In K. H. Rubin, W. M. Bukowski, & B. Laursen (Eds.), *Handbook of peer interactions, relationships, and groups* (pp. 473–489). New York, NY: Guilford Press.

Evans, G.W., & Kim, P. (2013). Childhood poverty, chronic stress, self-regulation, and coping. *Child Development Perspectives, 7*(1), 43–48.

Goldin-Meadow, S. (2006). How children learn language: A focus on resilience. In K. McCartney & D. Phillips (Eds.), *Handbook of early childhood development* (pp. 252–273). Malden, MA: Blackwell.

Howes, C. (2000). Social-emotional classroom climate in child care, child-teacher relationships and children's second grade peer relations. *Social Development, 9*(2), 191–204. doi:10.1111/1467-9507.00119

Karreman, A., van Tuijl, C., van Aken, M. A., & Deković, M. (2006). Parenting and self-regulation in preschoolers: A meta-analysis. *Infant and Child Development, 15*(6), 561–579.

Keogh, B. K. (1986). Temperament and schooling: Meaning of "goodness of fit." *New Directions for Child and Adolescent Development, 1986*(31), 89–108.

Keogh, B. K. (1994). Temperament and teachers' views of teachability. In W. B. Carey & S. C. McDevitt (Eds.), *Prevention and early intervention: Individual differences as risk factors for the mental health of children* (pp. 246–254). New York, NY: Brunner/Mazel.

McClelland, M. M., Ponitz, C. C., Messersmith, E. E., & Tominey, S. (2010). Self-regulation: The integration of cognition and emotion. In R. Lerner (Series Ed.) & W. Overton (Vol. Ed.), *Handbook of lifespan human development: Vol. 1. Cognition, biology and methods* (pp. 509–553). Hoboken, NJ: Wiley.

Phillips, D., McCartney, K., & Sussman, A. (2006). Child care and early development. In K. McCartney & D. Phillips (Eds.), *Blackwell handbook of early childhood development* (pp. 471–489). Malden, MA: Blackwell.

Raver, C. C., Jones, S. M., Li-Grining, C., Zhai, F., Bub, K., & Pressler, E. (2011). CSRP's impact on low-Income preschoolers' preacademic skills: Self-regulation as a mediating mechanism. *Child Development, 82*(1), 362–378. doi:10.1111/j.1467–8624.2010.01561.x

Rothbart, M. K., Posner, M. I., & Kieras, J. (2006). Temperament, attention, and the development of self-regulation. In K. McCartney & D. Phillips (Eds.), *Blackwell handbook of early childhood development* (pp. 338–357). Malden, MA: Blackwell.

Sanders, M. R., & Mazzucchelli, T. G. (2013). The promotion of self-regulation through parenting interventions. *Clinical Child and Family Psychology Review, 16*(1), 1–17.

Schneider, W., Schumann-Hengsteler, R., & Sodian, B. (2005). *Young children's cognitive development: Interrelationships among executive functioning, working memory, verbal ability, and theory of mind.* Mahwah, NJ: Erlbaum.

Sroufe, L. A. (1997). *Emotional development: The organization of emotional life in the early years.* Cambridge: Cambridge University Press.

Thomas, A., & Chess, S. (1986). The New York Longitudinal Study: From infancy to early adult life. In R. Plomin & J. Dunn (Eds.), *The study of temperament: Changes, continuities, and challenges* (pp. 39–52). Hillsdale, NJ: Erlbaum.

Williford, A. P., Vick Whittaker, J. E., Vitiello, V. E., & Downer, J. T. (2013). Children's engagement within the preschool classroom and their development of self-regulation. *Early Education & Development, 24*(2), 162–187.

3

● ● ● ● ●

Setting up the Classroom
for Self-Regulation Success

It was the beginning of a new school year and, like many teachers, Ms. Juliet was having a hard time with transitions throughout the school day. Getting a new group of children to cooperate during cleanup time was especially challenging. There were usually only two teachers in the room during this time to manage the "cleanup crew" of 20 children. Coming inside from the playground was also problematic. One child refused to come when called, and the amount of effort it took to help each child remove his or her rain gear without stepping on one another was exhausting! Transitions were not the only challenge Ms. Juliet faced. Circle time had also been a struggle. Children were having trouble sitting for the entire lesson. One child in particular was extremely active and often provoked those around him. The list of problematic behaviors in the classroom seemed to be growing each day. By the time Ms. Juliet left school at the end of each day, she was physically and mentally exhausted.

Starting a new school year with a brand new group of children who do not yet know or follow classroom routines can be challenging, even for a veteran teacher like Ms. Juliet. Without adequate self-regulation support and growth, the rest of the school year can be equally challenging!

Many of the challenges described in the foregoing scenario relate to regulation—the regulation of individual children, the regulation of the classroom as a whole, and even Ms. Juliet's own self-regulation. As we mentioned in Chapter 2, it is during the early childhood years that children experience a tremendous amount of growth in their self-regulation abilities, which can be seen as self-regulation begins to shift from an external to an internal process. For many early childhood teachers, this shift does not seem to happen soon enough! Importantly, early childhood classrooms and early childhood educators play a critical role in supporting children's ability to transition from external regulation to internal self-regulation because self-regulation skills must be taught and practiced (McClelland & Tominey, 2014). Teaching self-regulation skills throughout the day and providing children with increasingly complex activities and multiple opportunities to practice self-regulation during structured and unstructured activities as well as formal and informal learning times are critical to effectively supporting children's self-regulation growth and development (Diamond & Lee, 2011). In Chapter 2, we shared three ways that early childhood educators can lay a foundation for the development of self-regulation: (1) building secure relationships with children so that children feel safe and comfortable in the classroom and thus are better able to learn; (2) practicing self-regulation themselves so that children have models of these skills to observe and imitate; and (3) adopting an authoritative caregiving style, embedding language and approaches that promote critical thinking and perspective taking, and supporting the development of internal regulation. Building on this foundation, in this chapter, we discuss the importance of promoting self-regulation during the early childhood years and provide specific strategies and tips for teaching self-regulation in preschool.

● ● ● ● ●

The Importance of Supporting Self-Regulation Development in Early Childhood

As we discussed in Chapter 2, preschool is a critical time to help children practice and improve self-regulation skills because this is a period of significant developmental growth for children (McClelland, Ponitz, Messersmith, & Tominey, 2010). In addition, research shows that a substantial number of children struggle with self-regulation in early childhood. One study found that approximately 15% of children have difficulties with self-regulation and social skills during the transition from preschool to kindergarten (McClelland, Morrison, & Holmes, 2000). Another study suggests that as many as half of children enter kindergarten struggling with self-regulation (Rimm-Kaufman, Pianta, & Cox, 2000). Even when the majority of children in a classroom have adequate self-regulation skills, it can be extremely challenging to have even one or a few children in a class who have serious difficulties with these skills.

Self-Regulation as a Protective Factor for Children at Risk

Another reason promoting self-regulation in early childhood is so important is that self-regulation can serve as a protective factor, especially for children at risk (Obradovic, 2010; Sektnan, McClelland, Acock, & Morrison, 2010). A protective factor is an attribute or skill, like self-regulation, that helps an individual effectively manage stressful events or circumstances (Masten & Gewirtz, 2006). For example, one study found that children with strong self-regulation who were growing up in the context of risk (i.e., children living in poverty, children who were of ethnic minority status, and/or children who had mothers with chronic depression) had higher academic achievement in math, reading, and vocabulary than children with weaker self-regulation at the end of first grade (Sektnan et al., 2010). Another study found that self-regulation emerged as one of the strongest predictors of positive behavior and academic outcomes for children who were homeless (Obradovic, 2010). And finally, a third study found that self-regulation mediated the relationship between household chaos and children's externalizing behaviors (Hardaway, Wilson, Shaw, & Dishion, 2012). In other words, even though experiencing household chaos often relates to children having increased acting-out behaviors, children with stronger self-regulation who experienced chaos in their household had fewer instances of externalizing behaviors than their peers with poor self-regulation.

These findings suggest that self-regulation can buffer children against the stressful effects of risk, indicating that self-regulation may play a role in promoting resilience—the ability to have positive outcomes in the face of adversity (Masten & Gewirtz, 2006). With high numbers of children living in the context of risk (20% of all children in the U.S. live in poverty and 45% of children under five live in low-income families; Center for Law and Social Policy, 2014) promoting self-regulation in early childhood is one way that we can arm children with skills that will help them thrive despite the life challenges they may face. Unfortunately, research shows that children in at-risk situations are more likely than their peers to have self-regulation difficulties (Wanless, McClelland, Tominey, & Acock, 2011). Although this is concerning, there is strong evidence that, with support, self-regulation can be improved during preschool and that children who start behind their peers can catch up (Pears, Fisher, & Bronz, 2007; Tominey & McClelland, 2011).

● ● ● ● ●

Best Practices for Promoting Self-Regulation in Early Childhood

Research studies examining interventions aimed at promoting self-regulation and related skills (e.g., social competence) have identified several best practices for effectively teaching children new skills (Bierman & Erath, 2006; Diamond & Lee, 2011). To promote children's self-regulation, best practices include:

■ Modeling self-regulation by adults and peers and embedding self-regulation into classroom management practices;

- Teaching self-regulation skills, such as attention and inhibitory control, in a supportive environment and in developmentally appropriate ways;
- Increasing the complexity of children's self-regulation activities over time;
- Providing children with opportunities to practice self-regulation across different contexts;
- Giving children supportive feedback to guide them toward pro-social and well-regulated behaviors and strategies.

In Chapter 2, we discussed the importance of adults modeling and practicing self-regulation. In the next section, we will focus on the remaining best practices and provide specific tips for promoting self-regulation in early childhood classrooms using these best practices.

● ● ● ● ●

Embedding Self-Regulation Into Classroom Management Practices

Embedding self-regulation into classroom management practices is one important way that early childhood educators can support self-regulation development. Classroom management techniques can be used to provide external regulation for children, helping ensure smooth classroom functioning, while children are developing and learning the skills they need to make the shift to internal regulation. For example, research shows that teachers who help children anticipate what will happen throughout the day have children who make greater gains in self-regulation and academic achievement over the school year in comparison to children in classrooms where teachers do not provide this support (Cameron, Connor, & Morrison, 2005; Cameron & Morrison, 2011). In a study including preschool children, teachers who were better able to explain activities and the rationale behind them in whole-group settings had children who had higher scores on self-regulation and academic outcomes at the end of the school year in comparison to teachers who did not (Cameron & Morrison, 2011). This type of classroom management and organization can lay the foundation for effective self-regulation and learning by helping children identify and focus on the relevant activities, ignore distractions, and engage in behavior needed for specific tasks. Together these studies suggest that classroom management has an impact not only on self-regulation but also on children's academic outcomes.

Let's take a look at a typical early childhood classroom schedule (see Table 3.1).

Table 3.1 Example of a Typical Early Childhood Classroom Daily Schedule

Time	Activity
8:00–9:30 a.m.	Arrival and individual play
9:30–10:00 a.m.	Morning meeting (group time/circle time)
10:00–10:45 a.m.	Learning centers and small groups
10:45–11:00 a.m.	Snack
11:00–11:45 a.m.	Outdoor time
11:45–12:00 p.m.	Music and movement
12:00–12:40 p.m.	Lunch and cleanup
12:40–1:00 p.m.	Story and toileting
1:00–3:00 p.m.	Rest time
3:00–3:30 p.m.	Wake up, toileting, and individual play
3:30–3:45 p.m.	Snack
3:45–4:30 p.m.	Outdoor time
4:30–5:00 p.m.	Stories and home

In Table 3.1, we can see many opportunities throughout the day in which self-regulation can be embedded. Not only can self-regulation be embedded in activities, but also it can play an important role in helping educators and children navigate the transitions from one activity to another. Transitions are often cited by early childhood educators as being one of the most challenging parts of the day.

Learning Checkpoint #1

1. Make a list of all the transitions children experience during a typical preschool day (e.g., entering the classroom and transitioning from home to school, cleaning up after individual play, going from inside to outside).

    a. Which of these transitions do you find to be the most challenging in your classroom? What strategies can teachers use to help children navigate these transitions smoothly? What strategies do you use to help children in your classroom navigate transitions smoothly?

Ms. Melissa greets each child and family as they arrive at school in the morning. Next to the classroom door, she has posted a series of pictures showing children in the classroom going through the morning routine (e.g., hanging a coat in a cubby, washing hands). She encourages children to use the pictures to guide their actions and show their families what they do as they settle in each morning. As children begin playing in the various areas of the classroom, Ms. Melissa checks in with individual children to ask how they are feeling and spends a little extra time with children who seem to be having unpleasant feelings. She asks about their morning, gives a hug to those who are feeling sad, and helps them find activities they like to engage in. Ms. Melissa also spends time with each small group of children, guiding them through interactions with one another by providing them with the words they need to say: "May I have that when you're done?" and "Please stop. I don't like it when you do that." Ms. Melissa carefully plans each circle time. She chooses activities that allow children hands-on opportunities and makes sure the activities she chooses are short and engaging. She also chooses activities that allow children to practice self-regulation abilities, including turn taking and starting and stopping to various cues (e.g., freeze dancing). At the end of circle time and throughout the day, Ms. Melissa takes time to explain to children what is going to happen next to prepare them for the transition, helping them understand their choices, and providing them with guidance as to what is expected of them. As the day continues, Ms. Melissa monitors the energy level of children in her class so that she can choose transition activities that help them shift from a high-energy level to a low-energy level or from low to high. For example, Ms. Melissa noticed that following outside time, children had trouble transitioning to sitting at the lunch table. One day she tried adding a music and movement activity in between outdoor time and lunchtime, which started with high-energy dancing and ended with yoga poses and deep breaths. She noticed that this activity worked so well to help children manage the transition inside that she made it a regular part of her daily schedule. At the end of lunch, Ms. Melissa dims the lights and turns on quiet music to help provide children with cues indicating that rest time is coming and to help regulate children's energy levels.

In this scenario, Ms. Melissa demonstrates many different ways that she supports children's self-regulation development throughout the day. Ms. Melissa provides external regulation by planning activities into transitions and helping children anticipate and prepare for what is coming next. Ms. Melissa also directly teaches self-regulation skills through guiding children's interactions with one another and providing them with opportunities to practice self-regulation during informal conversations and formal learning opportunities, including during circle time.

● ● ● ● ●

Teaching Self-Regulation Through Circle Time

Circle time (also called "morning meeting" or "large group time") is an important part of the preschool day. In most classrooms, circle time is an opportunity for all children and teachers to come together for a shared lesson or activity. Although children learn throughout the day in many different ways, circle time is considered to be one of the primary "formal" learning opportunities within a typical preschool day. Providing children with opportunities to practice stopping, thinking, and then acting through fun and engaging activities that are outside of emotionally charged situations (see "Activity Break #1") helps children practice these skills so that they will be better able to self-regulate in moments that are emotionally charged (e.g., when in the middle of a conflict with another child).

● ● ● ● ●

Providing Opportunities to Practice Self-Regulation: Classroom Transitions

In addition to circle time, there are many other instances throughout the day when educators can teach children self-regulation skills. Educators who manage transitions well by providing children support through external regulation (e.g., singing a song with children) are also teaching children valuable skills that can turn into internal self-regulation in the future. A research study found that children who participated in community music classes had higher self-regulation on a variety of self-regulation tasks than children from a similar demographic who had not participated in community music (Winsler, Ducenne, & Koury, 2011). One of the observations made during the study was that when children participated in tasks that required them to wait, those who had taken music classes sang to themselves to pass the time. This suggests that music classes helped teach children a strategy (singing) that children were able to use to entertain themselves when they had to wait, such as during this study. Waiting is a challenge for young children. In fact, waiting can be a challenge for adults! The next time you are standing in a line, riding on a bus, or doing something that requires waiting in public for any period of time, look at the adults around you to see how they are managing this waiting time. Some adults will wait quietly humming or thinking to themselves, others will engage in conversation with those around them, and still others will use a portable electronic device (e.g., smartphone) to entertain themselves. Just like adults, children have an easier time waiting if they have something to keep themselves occupied during that time. Teachers can help provide children with strategies of things to do when they need to wait.

● ● ● ● ●

Providing Supportive Feedback That Fosters Self-Regulation Growth and Development

Just like any other skill (e.g., learning to read, cutting with scissors), learning self-regulation is a process. Self-regulation is a skill that must be taught, practiced, and developed. Imagine a child, Logan, who is struggling to cut a straight line with scissors. When Logan asks for help, his teacher, Ms. Judy, sits down next to him and helps him put his fingers properly into the scissor grip (he was holding the scissors backwards initially). She then uses a hand-over-hand approach to guide his hand and scissors down the line. As Logan tries again and again, Ms. Judy continues to help Logan cut, but slowly provides him with less support over time. Ms. Judy also gives Logan additional pieces of paper and different shapes to cut out to help him gain confidence in his cutting abilities and use them in new and different ways.

How do you think learning to cut with scissors is similar to the process children go through to learn self-regulation? How do you think it is different?

A few similarities between learning to cut with scissors and learning self-regulation are that children need to be taught how to demonstrate both of these skills, they need support from an adult or peer who is more skilled than they are, and they need practice in lots of different contexts. What if rather than struggling with cutting, Logan was struggling with self-regulation at the art table? Imagine that when Logan sat down at the art table, Logan grabbed a pair of scissors from another child, Isaac, who was sitting next to him. Isaac cried out, "Hey! That's mine!" and tried to take the scissors back from Logan. Logan pushed Isaac away and cut a perfectly straight line right down the middle of Isaac's art project.

One primary difference that we can see between the two scenarios is that when Logan was having trouble cutting a straight line on his own, Logan's struggles were not disruptive to others around him. The same would be true if Logan was having difficulties remembering which lowercase letter (d or b) was the letter "B." His teacher might take note that Logan called out the wrong letter during circle time, but probably would not need to stop the activity to address this challenge with Logan individually. Instead, she would work with him on letter recognition at another time. In the scenario where Logan struggles with self-regulation, however, he requires immediate attention from a teacher to help him stop his behavior that is related to a breakdown in self-regulation (e.g., grabbing scissors from another child, pushing). Not only will Logan's teacher want to support Logan by helping him practice a better regulated and more pro-social behavior (e.g., helping him use words to ask for a turn), but also she will be anxious to prevent his behavior from escalating in the moment and want to ensure that she is available to support an emotional response that arises from Logan or Isaac in the situation.

Interestingly, the example with Logan mirrors the way that many teachers think about self-regulation. Surveys of kindergarten teachers have found that teachers report self-regulation skills as those most helpful for children when they enter kindergarten more often than they cite academic skills (Rimm-Kaufman et al., 2000). This is likely because when children struggle with self-regulation skills, it is more disruptive to the learning environment than when children have struggles with early academic skills. Studies have shown that poor self-regulation relates to classroom behavior problems and difficulties interacting effectively with others (Eisenberg, Eggum, Sallquist, & Edwards, 2010; Garner & Waajid, 2012).

● ● ● ● ●
Learning Checkpoint #2

How do you know when children in your class are struggling with self-regulation? How do you typically give children feedback when they have a breakdown in self-regulation? What opportunities do you provide children who are struggling with self-regulation to practice and improve self-regulation skills?

From very young ages, children who demonstrate difficulties with self-regulation are at risk of being labeled as the child who cannot sit still, the child who cannot pay attention, the child who hits, the child who yells, the child who tantrums, the challenging child, the bad child. The way that adults, including educators, respond to a child's breakdown in self-regulation can turn a child's struggles with self-regulation into learning opportunities or a perpetuating cycle of dis-regulation. The response from adults also shapes the way other children learn to respond to a child who is having difficulties.

Consider the following scenario:

Emily is known in her classroom as being the child who pushes. Even the other children will say things like, "I don't want to be by Emily. She always pushes me!"

One day, as the children are lining up to go outside, Emily pushes her way to the front of the line. Ms. Serena takes Emily's hand and leads her to the back of the line. She points out to Emily that there were other children already waiting in line and that Emily's friends did not like being pushed. A boy in front of Emily named Roger turns and says, "I don't like you." Ms. Serena says to Roger, "Emily is having an attitude again. Just ignore her." She then turns to Emily and says, "See. Other people don't like it you when you do things like that. Stand here and hold my hand until everyone else is outside, and then you can go too."

By leading Emily to the back of the line, Ms. Serena is providing external regulation for Emily's actions. She is also removing Emily from the situation and missing an opportunity to help her practice standing in line or asking for a space in line in a pro-social and self-regulated way. What message do you think Ms. Serena is sending to Roger with her words? What message is she sending to Emily?

What if Ms. Serena had handled the situation differently?

Roger turns and says, "I don't like you." Ms. Serena says to Roger, "Roger, did you feel upset when Emily pushed you?" Roger nodded. Ms. Serena says to him, "You could tell Emily, 'I don't like it when you do that.'" Roger does and Emily looks down. Ms. Serena helps Emily ask Roger, "May I stand next to you?" and then stays nearby to make sure Emily's behaviors remain pro-social. Ms. Serena says out loud to both Roger and Emily, "Standing in line and waiting for a turn is really hard, isn't it? Sometimes I just want to push right to the front, but even I have to remind myself to wait for my turn."

In the second scenario, Ms. Serena not only takes advantage of this opportunity to provide Emily with external regulation but also teaches Emily the self-regulation skills she needs to navigate the situation in the future. Importantly, she also acknowledges that self-regulation is a skill that needs to be practiced and developed and that this process is normal—for Emily and even for herself. In the second scenario, Ms. Serena's words tell Roger that Emily is working on self-regulation—not that Emily is a bad child. Once an adult begins labeling a child (e.g., "He is always causing problems" or "She has an attitude"), a shift can occur that hinders the ability of the adult to effectively help and teach the child. Research on interventions suggests that providing children with supportive feedback and giving them the opportunity to modify their words or behavior and try again are most effective (Bierman & Erath, 2006).

● ● ● ● ●

Tips for Promoting Self-Regulation in Early Childhood Classrooms

1. *Embed self-regulation into classroom management practices.*
   a. Create and maintain a classroom schedule. Children thrive on routine, and having a consistent pattern from one day to the next helps children anticipate what is coming, which supports their ability to self-regulate across the school day.
   b. Provide visual cues that help children learn and follow the classroom schedule. For example, display a classroom schedule that includes pictures showing children engaging in each activity across the day (e.g., circle time, hand washing, playing outside). Draw children's attention throughout the day to teach children

how to "read" the pictures and understand how to tell what is coming next. Encourage children to use the schedule to tell their parents about their day during pickup or drop-off. Providing visual cues is also an important support for children who are dual language learners!

c. Use oral cues throughout the day to remind children of the routine. Oral cues might include spoken words (e.g., "Five more minutes until clean up time!") or songs (e.g., "Clean up, clean up, everybody everywhere."). Music is typically a very effective method for engaging children in transitions and activities. Integrating songs throughout the day about cleaning up, lining up, getting ready for lunch, preparing for nap, and so on provides children with a comforting reminder of what is coming next and one that they can participate in by singing along!

d. Set up the classroom environment to support self-regulation success. Think about the way your classroom is set up to support children's ability to regulate across the day, and consider ways that you can modify the environment. For example, simple ways of modifying the environment involve dimming the lights at rest time to help children move from a high- to a low-energy state. Playing different kinds of music at different times of day (e.g., classical music during quiet activities) can set the tone for the environment. Finally, physically rearranging the classroom can also have an impact on children's regulation abilities.

2. *Intentionally teach self-regulation in fun and engaging ways, using games that become increasingly complex.*

a. Play self-regulation games during circle time, outdoor time, music and movement, or other times throughout the day. The "Activity Breaks" presented throughout this book provide specific examples of games that can be used with children individually as well as in small and large groups, with modifications for making the games increasingly complex as children learn the basic rules.

3. *Provide children with opportunities to practice self-regulation across different contexts.*

a. Use pictures to help children self-regulate in different areas of the classroom and while participating in different activities. For example, if only four children are allowed in the block area at a time, place a picture of four children (or stick figures) next to the block area. Explain to children that the picture means that only four children can play in that area. When you see children go to the block area, point out the picture and say, "Let's see how many people can play with the blocks at one time," and count the people in the picture together. Next, count the children in the area together: "One, two, three. It looks like there are only three children, so you can play too!" With time, children will learn to stop, count, and regulate their behavior themselves (choosing to join in or find another activity).

b. Teach children songs, fingerplays, or games that they can sing and play while transitioning or waiting. Model singing a song while waiting in line with children (e.g., "It looks like we have to wait for our turn. Maybe we should sing a song while we wait. What song would you like to sing?").

4. *Give children supportive feedback.*

a. Provide warm and supportive feedback. When providing children with feedback, choose words that communicate the message that children are working on a skill that takes time and practice. Use words that express to children that you care about them, but did not care for a specific behavior. By focusing on a child's behavior ("I don't like it when you yell in my ear"), acknowledging the child's feelings ("It looks like you are feeling impatient and you were trying to get my attention"), providing children with positive alternatives ("When you want someone's attention, you can say, 'Will you help me please?'"), and then giving children an opportunity to try that behavior, you help children practice regulation skills in an environment where they feel supported, rather than shamed, making it more likely they will look to you for modeling, guidance, and support in the future.

b. Reframe the way children in your classroom view one another. An important part of setting up a supportive classroom environment is fostering supportive relationships between children. When children witness another child having a breakdown in self-regulation (e.g., a child pushes another child or has a temper tantrum), children will often say things like, "I don't like him" or "She's mean." Explain to children that their friend is learning how to be a good friend and that we all have to help each other. Ask children what they do to be good friends, and give them opportunities to show these skills to one another.

Reflect

Think back to the scenario presented earlier in this chapter with Emily and Ms. Serena. Which of the scenarios with Emily is most similar to your own approach with children—the first or the second? How can you help children in your classroom approach one another with understanding and support, even when they demonstrate a breakdown in self-regulation? What specific words would you use?

Set a Goal

Choose at least two ideas presented in this chapter or in "Activity Break #1: Circle Time Games to Promote Self-Regulation," which follows this chapter, to try with children in your own classroom. Make a plan for adding the activities you selected to your classroom lesson plan.

After trying them out, reflect on the following: How did children respond to the activity that you chose? What did you like about the activity? Did you experience any challenges with the activities you chose? If so, how would you modify them in the future?

● ● ● ● ●

Additional Resources

See Chapter 9 for additional resources related to the contents of this chapter, including Internet resources focusing on integrating self-regulation in the early childhood classroom and recommended children's books focusing on self-regulation.

● ● ● ● ●

References

Bierman, K. L., & Erath, S. A. (2006). Promoting social competence in early childhood: Classroom curricula and social skills coaching programs. In K. McCartney & D. Phillips (Eds.), *Blackwell handbook of early childhood development* (pp. 595–615). Malden, MA: Blackwell.

Cameron, C. E., Connor, C. M., & Morrison, F. J. (2005). Effects of variation in teacher organization on classroom functioning. *Journal of School Psychology, 43,* 61–85.

Cameron, C. E., & Morrison, F. J. (2011). Teacher activity orienting predicts preschoolers' academic and self-regulatory skills. *Early Education & Development, 22,* 620–648.

Center for Law and Social Policy. (2014). New census data tell us that poverty fell in 2013. Retrieved November 17, 2014, from www.clasp.org/issues/child-care-and-early-education/in-focus/2013-poverty-data-a-glimpse-of-good-news-for-children-but-we-can-do-better

Diamond, A., & Lee, K. (2011). Interventions shown to aid executive function development in children 4 to 12 years old. *Science, 333*(6045), 959–964.

Eisenberg, N., Eggum, N. D., Sallquist, J., & Edwards, A. (2010). Relations of self-regulatory/control capacities to maladjustment, social competence, and emotionality. In R. H. Hoyle (Ed.), *Handbook of personality and self-regulation* (pp. 19–46). Oxford: Wiley-Blackwell.

Garner, P. W., & Waajid, B. (2012). Emotion knowledge and self-regulation as predictors of preschoolers' cognitive ability, classroom behavior, and social competence. *Journal of Psychoeducational Assessment, 30*(4), 330–343.

Hardaway, C. R., Wilson, M. N., Shaw, D. S., & Dishion, T. J. (2012). Family functioning and externalizing behaviour among low-income children: Self-regulation as a mediator. *Infant and Child Development, 21*(1), 67–84.

Masten, A. S., & Gewirtz, A. H. (2006). Vulnerability and resilience in early child development. In K. McCartney & D. Phillips (Eds.), *Blackwell handbook of early childhood development* (pp. 22–43). Malden, MA: Blackwell.

McClelland, M. M., Morrison, F. J., & Holmes, D. L. (2000). Children at-risk for early academic problems: The role of learning-related social skills. *Early Childhood Research Quarterly, 15*, 307–329. doi:10.1016/S0885–2006(00)00069–7

McClelland, M. M., Ponitz, C. C., Messersmith, E. E., & Tominey, S. (2010). Self-regulation: The integration of cognition and emotion. In R. Lerner (Series Ed.) & W. Overton (Vol. Ed.), *Handbook of lifespan human development: Vol. 1. Cognition, biology and methods* (pp. 509–553). Hoboken, NJ: Wiley.

McClelland, M. M., & Tominey, S. L. (2014). The development of self-regulation and executive function in young children. *Zero to Three Journal, 35*(2), 2–8.

Obradovic, J. (2010). Effortful control and adaptive functioning of homeless children: Variable-focused and person-focused analyses. *Journal of Applied Developmental Psychology, 31*(2), 109–117. doi:10.1016/j.appdev.2009.09.004

Pears, K. C., Fisher, P. A., & Bronz, K. D. (2007). An intervention to facilitate school readiness in foster children: Preliminary results from the Kids in Transition to School pilot study. *School Psychology Review, 36*(4), 665–673.

Rimm-Kaufman, S., Pianta, R. C., & Cox, M. J. (2000). Teachers' judgments of problems in the transition to kindergarten. *Early Childhood Research Quarterly, 15*(2), 147–166.

Sektnan, M., McClelland, M. M., Acock, A., & Morrison, F. J. (2010). Relations between early family risk, children's behavioral regulation, and academic achievement. *Early Childhood Research Quarterly, 25*(4), 464–479. doi:10.1016/j.ecresq.2010.02.005

Tominey, S. L., & McClelland, M. M. (2011). Red light, purple light: Findings from a randomized trial using circle time games to improve behavioral self-regulation in preschool. *Early Education and Development, 22*(3), 489–519.

Wanless, S. B., McClelland, M. M., Tominey, S. L., & Acock, A. (2011). The influence of demographic risk factors on the development of behavioral regulation in prekindergarten and kindergarten. *Early Education and Development, 22*(3), 461–488.

Winsler, A., Ducenne, L., & Koury, A. (2011). Singing one's way to self-regulation: The role of early music and movement curricula and private speech. *Early Education and Development, 22*(2), 274–304.

ACTIVITY BREAK #1: CIRCLE TIME GAMES TO PROMOTE SELF-REGULATION

In this activity break, we present activities and games that can be used during circle time to help children practice and develop self-regulation in fun and engaging ways. They are intended to help children practice the core components of self-regulation (i.e., attentional flexibility, working memory, and inhibitory control) in fun and engaging ways so that children develop the skills they need to stop, think, and then act. Many of these activities can be used outside of circle time as well, including during small group time, during music and movement, or even during transitions. Some of these games can even be modified for use with individual children.

Conductor

(Circle time or small group)

Materials:

- A set of classroom musical instruments (or homemade musical instruments—e.g., shakers, or jingle bell bracelets)
- A conducting baton (dowel rod or pencil).

Procedure: Give each child an instrument. Tell them that you (the teacher) are a conductor and they are the orchestra. When the conductor waves the baton, the orchestra plays their instruments. When the conductor sets the baton down, the orchestra stops playing. When the conductor waves the baton, the orchestra plays again. Rather than playing instruments, you can ask children to move their bodies in this game (e.g., clapping their hands or stomping their feet). *Helpful hint:* Children will be eager to play their musical instruments as soon as they have them in hand. Before passing out instruments, think about the expectations that you have for children when they receive their instruments and take time to communicate those expectations. You may find it helpful to explain the instructions for the conductor game before passing out the instruments and allow children to play their instruments as soon as they receive them, practicing stopping when you put down the baton for the first time. When using this activity with a small group, give children the opportunity to be the conductor as well. They will enjoy watching their classmates' respond to their movements and cues.

Skill development: This activity helps children practice attention by requiring them to focus on the conductor, practice working memory by asking children to remember which cues represent start and stop or fast or slow (especially when you play variations #1 and #2), and practice inhibitory control by encouraging children to start and stop intentionally. Children are also developing musicality and practicing fine and gross motor skills in this activity.

Conductor Variation #1

Make this game more challenging by having children play their instruments quickly or slowly based on the speed of the conductor's baton. Additionally, try the opposite game—ask children to play their instruments when the conductor sets his or her baton down and stop playing while the conductor is waving the baton. Try having children play loudly when you wave the baton up high in the air and softly when you wave the baton down low near the ground.

Conductor Variation #2

Add another cue that children must watch for when the conductor waves his or her baton. For example, tell children to play their instruments when the conductor touches his nose *and* waves the baton, but not to play their instruments when the conductor is only waving the baton. See Figure 3.1 for an image of a child playing Conductor.

Figure 3.1 A Child Playing Conductor.
Photo by Shauna Tominey.

It's Raining, It's Pouring

(Circle time or small group)

Materials: None.

Procedure: Tell children that you are going to create a pretend rainstorm together by making different sounds with your hands and voice. Show children all of the different sounds and actions that you are going to use first. Allow children to copy you as you demonstrate.
  Steps to creating a rainstorm:

1. Rub your hands together, and make a whispered whooshing sound with your voice to make the sound of the wind.
2. Snap your fingers lightly or tap the fingers together on each hand to make a sound like raindrops.
3. Clap your hands slowly at first and then more quickly to represent rain.
4. Pat your knees or the floor or stomp your feet to make the sound of a heavy rainstorm. Use your voice to add thunder sounds.

After introducing the sounds and actions to your class, ask them to copy you as you make a rainstorm all together. Start with slow, quiet actions to build your own rainstorm, beginning with the wind, working through steps 1–4, and ending with a heavy rainstorm. Then lead children backwards through the steps, ending with the wind blowing the last few raindrops away.

Skill development: This game helps children practice paying attention to visual and oral cues. Children also practice inhibitory control skills by switching from one action to another in response to those cues and build fine and gross motor skills.

Introducing the Classroom Pet (Puppet)

(Circle time)

Materials:

■ A stuffed animal puppet.

Procedure: Hold the puppet behind your back, and tell children that you have a new friend (or classroom pet) to introduce to them. (Note that it is okay to tell children that the pet is just a puppet and that you are pretending it is real.) Let children know that the new pet is feeling a little scared about being in a new place and gets startled easily by loud noises and voices. Ask children if they would like to hold or touch the new pet. Take a few deep breaths together as a class to help everyone calm their bodies, practice whispering to demonstrate quiet voices, and show children how to touch the pet with gentle hands. Walk around the circle, and give each child a chance to hold and touch the new pet. The classroom pet can join the circle during quiet activities (e.g., yoga or shared reading) and can serve as a concrete reminder that this is an activity where we need to show calm in our bodies.

Skill development: This activity lays a foundation for emotion regulation by helping children experience the feeling of calm and practice strategies for bringing their body to a calm state (e.g., deep breathing). In this activity, children also practice paying attention, following directions, and taking turns.

Listening Bingo

(Circle time or small group)

Materials:

■ Audio recorder (e.g., voice recorder on a smartphone).

Procedure: Create a recording of various sounds from around your home or the classroom (e.g., door closing, phone ringing, running water from the sink, toilet flushing, vacuum cleaner). You can also create a recording of children in your classroom saying a word ("hello") or a short phrase ("Guess who?"). Share the recording with children during small or large group time, and ask them to guess what or whom they are hearing. You can also show pictures of the different sounds children might hear or give them clues that help them identify the different sounds.

Skill development: This activity provides children an opportunity to pay attention to audio sounds and tap into their working memory to recall sounds that they have heard in the past. Asking children questions about the sounds that they hear can help them build their critical thinking abilities ("Is it a high sound or a low sound?" "Have you heard a sound like this before?").

Mirror, Mirror

(Circle time, gross motor activity, or small group)

Chant:

"Mirror, mirror, look and see. Everybody copy me."

Materials:

■ Hand mirror (optional).

Procedure: Stand up in front of the class, and tell children you are going to play a game where you are pretending to look in the mirror and they (the children) are your reflection. Ask them to copy everything you do just like a mirror. You can use a hand mirror to demonstrate. If using this activity with a small group, have children stand in pairs facing one another. Hand one child in each pair a block or other token, and tell children that who-ever is holding the token moves first, while the other person tries to copy them. After a few minutes, have children switch roles.

Skill development: This activity helps children practice attentional flexibility by encouraging them to pay attention to and copy the move-ments of the teacher or their partner. Children also practice spatial awareness, fine and gross motor skills, and turn taking.

Music Maps

(Circle time, music and movement, small group)

Materials:

■ Construction paper or butcher paper (one piece of construction paper per child or a large enough piece of butcher paper to accom-modate the group)
■ Markers or crayons (one per child).

Procedure: Explain to children that you will be drawing along to music and that they can draw any way that they like. If children in your class-room are at a developmental level where they are able to follow more complex sets of directions, ask children to try to draw without lifting up their marker or crayon so that they draw one continuous line/scribble. You can also ask children to try to follow along with the music (drawing quickly during fast parts and slowly during slow parts). Try this activity several times on different days, using different types of music.

Skill development: In this activity, children attend to musical cues to help guide fine motor and gross motor responses. Children are devel-oping musicality and artistic skills while also practicing inhibitory control through modifying their actions based on aural cues.

Musical Simon Says

(Circle time, gross motor activity, music and movement, or small group)

Materials:

■ Three musical instruments (e.g., a shaker, a bell, and a drum; alter-native: use snapping, clapping, and stomping).

Procedure: Show children the three musical instruments that you chose, and let them hear the sound of each one. Choose an action that children can do along with the sound of each instrument. For example, ask children to shake their hands in the air when you shake the shaker and freeze when you stop. After practicing with one instrument a few times, add another instrument. Ask children to stomp their feet when you ring the bell and freeze when you stop. Now put the two instruments together so that children have to shake their hands in response to the shaker, stomp their feet in response to the bell, freeze when you stop, or perform both actions when you play both instruments at the same time. If children are able follow these instructions, make the game more challenging by adding a third instrument! If playing in small groups, children can be given the opportunity to choose actions to correspond with the instruments or even lead the activity by playing the instruments and leading their peers in starting and stopping.

Skill development: This activity helps children practice each of the components of self-regulation, including attention to attend to the visual and aural cues provided by the circle time leader, working memory in order to remember the actions that correspond with each instrument, and inhibitory control to start and stop their actions in response to cues. They are also practicing vocabulary, musicality and rhythm, and fine and gross motor skills.

Mystery Bag

(Circle time or small group)

Materials:

- Brown paper bag
- 1–3 items (items from around the classroom or from the outdoors).

Procedure: Place one of the mystery items in the bag when children are not watching. Bring the bag with the item inside to circle time or small group time. Tell children that you have something hiding in the bag and you are going to play a guessing game to see if they can figure out what it is. Help children think of questions to ask that will help them figure out what is inside the bag (e.g., "I wonder what else you could ask. Do you know what color the mystery item is? Do you know if it is an animal with two legs or four legs?"). Write words and draw pictures (if you are artistically inclined) showing what they have learned so far on a large piece of paper or easel. When playing this game in small groups, give children the opportunity to hide an item in the bag and answer questions asked by their peers.

Skill development: This game helps children develop attention skills through paying attention to the conversation and line of questions related to the mystery item. Children have to practice attentional flexibility by turning their attention from the teacher to peers and inhibitory control through turn taking. Children are also developing conversation and deductive reasoning skills.

Sleeping, Sleeping, all the Children are Sleeping

(Circle time, gross motor activity, music and movement, small group)

Materials: None.

Procedure: To begin this game, explain to children that their places in the circle (e.g., mats or carpet squares) are now "beds" where they can pretend to sleep whenever they hear the *Sleeping Song*. Chant or sing the *Sleeping Song*: "*Sleeping, sleeping, all the children are sleeping*," and ask children to practice going to sleep. Tell children that each time they hear the song, they should return to their "bed" to sleep. Once children are pretending to sleep, wake them up by saying, "And when they woke up . . . they were *butterflies*!" Children can now fly around the room, flapping their arms like butterfly wings! Each time you sing the *Sleeping Song*, it's time for children to return to their mats and pretend to sleep again. Replace "butterflies" with other animals or actions (e.g., "jumping up and down" or "driving a fire truck"). Actions can be chosen that correspond with classroom themes (e.g., "stomping like a tyrannosaurus" or "eating leaves like a stegosaurus" for a dinosaur theme), and you can sing the *Sleeping Song* multiple times in a row if needed to allow children time to return to their "beds." You can also ask children for ideas for animals or actions.

Skill development: This game focuses on inhibitory control, although each aspect of self-regulation is included. For instance, children practice cognitive flexibility by paying attention to cues that let them know when to sleep and when to wake up as well as the teacher's instructions. Children need to use working memory to remember the instructions for the game and inhibitory control to stop one action to participate in another. In addition, the sleeping game promotes vocabulary development (learning about new actions in connection with classroom themes), fine and gross motor skills (moving their bodies in imitation of animals and actions), and spatial awareness (monitoring the space around themselves and gaining awareness of other children).

Sleeping Game Variation #1

Procedure: To help children practice higher levels of self-regulatory skills, try providing wake-up cues in different ways. Rather than *saying* the name of an animal or action, act out an animal or action that children must guess before joining in. In this variation, children are required to stop, look up, and think about the teacher's movements before participating.

Sleeping Game Variation #2

Materials:

■ Three pieces of different colored construction paper (e.g., red, yellow, and blue) with pictures of animals on one side.

Procedure: Paste pictures of three animals onto three pieces of colored construction paper (e.g., a snake on red paper, an elephant on green paper, a monkey on yellow paper). After singing the *Sleeping Song*, point to one of the pictures. Children must look up to see which picture has been selected before acting. After playing a few rounds, turn the papers over so that children can see the colors of the papers, but not the animal pictures. Play the game, asking children if they can remember which animal is represented by each color (e.g., "I'm pointing to the blue circle—do you remember what animal was on the blue?"). This variation encourages children to practice attention and memory skills in order to remember which animal corresponds with each color.

4

●●●●●

Self-Regulation and Circle Time

Five minutes before the end of individual play and exploration, Ms. Melissa sang out, "Five more minutes, listen everyone. Five more minutes, then playtime will be done!" At the end of the five minutes, Ms. Melissa started singing the classroom cleanup song, and many children joined in. They also joined her in putting activities away, including stacking blocks, returning babies to the dramatic play area, and hanging up easels. Ms. Melissa knew which children would have the most difficulty leaving their activity to clean up and positioned herself next to them to redirect and guide them as she started singing. When the room was mostly put back together, Ms. Melissa moved to the circle time rug, allowing her assistant teacher, Ms. Michelle, to continue helping the last few children. Ms. Melissa had already spread out carpet squares with children's names on them around the circle time area. She turned on her class's favorite dance song and invited children to come to join her on the rug. Children came to the rug dancing, jumping, and spinning in circles. Ms. Melissa reminded them that their carpet squares were their "safe" spots and the rug was hot lava! She helped children untangle from the middle of the rug to get out of the hot lava and dance on their safe squares. When the song ended, Ms. Melissa and the children remained standing as they reached up toward the ceiling as far as they could to reach an imaginary hose. They pulled the hose down and with a "Pssssshhhhhhh" washed all the hot lava away. They reached back up to put the hose away and sat down on their carpet squares. Ms. Melissa and the children took a few deep breaths together, and they continued the rest of their circle time routine.

As we discussed in Chapter 3, circle time may be the only "formal" learning opportunity that occurs during the preschool day, and this time can be used to promote children's learning on a range of topics, including self-regulation. What happens before and after circle time, however, can be as critical as what happens during this time. In order for children to take advantage of the social, emotional, and academic learning activities that occur as part of circle time, they must be ready to engage in learning. Giving children an opportunity to calm down and refocus prior to circle time, like Ms. Melissa did, can help children pay attention and take advantage of the learning environment. In addition, circle time routines help children know what to expect and ensure that activities are interesting and meaningful to children, are developmentally appropriate, allow children the opportunity to participate, and are not too long. All these factors are essential to running a successful and well-regulated circle time.

In this chapter, we talk about the importance of circle time as an opportunity for teaching self-regulation and allowing children opportunities to practice these skills. We present an overview and findings from a preschool intervention—the Kindergarten Readiness Study – that uses circle time games to help children practice and develop self-regulation skills. We also present "Ten Tips for a Well-Regulated Circle Time" and conclude with songs that can be integrated into circle time routines to support transitioning in and out of circle time.

• • • • •

Early Childhood Self-Regulation Interventions

There are many interventions that have been developed in recent years aimed at promoting aspects of children's self-regulation. These interventions include classroom curricula, such as Tools of the Mind (Diamond, Barnett, Thomas, & Munro, 2007), comprehensive programs, such as PATHS (Promoting Alternative Thinking Strategies), the Kids in Transition to School Program (Pears, Fisher, Bruce, Kim, & Yoerger, 2010), the Chicago School Readiness Project (Raver et al., 2011), and Preschool RULER (Rivers, Tominey, O'Bryon, & Brackett, 2013), and more focused programs, such as the Kindergarten Readiness Study (Schmitt, McClelland, Tominey, & Acock, 2015; Tominey & McClelland, 2011, 2013). Each of these intervention programs focus on improving different aspects of self-regulation and provide different types of support for self-regulation growth. In this chapter, we focus on one of these intervention programs, the Kindergarten Readiness Study, because it is this intervention that served as the foundation for this book and many of the activities that we present. In Chapter 9, we include a list of additional interventions and provide related websites where you can learn more about these other programs.

• • • • •

The Kindergarten Readiness Study

The Kindergarten Readiness Study focuses on a set of circle time games that are designed to help children practice self-regulation in fun and engaging ways (Tominey & McClelland, 2011). Each of the games includes music and movement to facilitate children's engagement (Tominey & McClelland, 2013). All of the circle time games used in the Kindergarten Readiness Study are easy for teachers to learn and implement during circle time, and all of them are included in this book (see Table 9.1 for a complete list of games).

● ● ● ● ●

Results From the Kindergarten Readiness Study

Two randomized control studies have been conducted focused on the Kindergarten Readiness Study to date. The first study included 65 preschoolers, half of whom were from low-income families. Children in the first pilot study were randomly chosen to participate in either an intervention group or a control group. The intervention group participated in self-regulation circle time games twice weekly for eight weeks. Findings from this pilot study showed that children who started the year with low self-regulation scores and who participated in the intervention had greater gains in self-regulation than children who started the year with low self-regulation scores in the control group (Tominey & McClelland, 2011, 2013). These findings provide evidence that children's self-regulatory skills are malleable and that children who start preschool with poor self-regulation can show significant improvement in these skills with support and intervention! Children who participated in the intervention group also showed significantly greater gains in early reading skills than children in the control group. We will discuss this finding in more detail in Chapter 5.

A second study was conducted with 276 low-income preschoolers, all of whom were enrolled in Head Start. As in the first study, children were randomly assigned to receive the intervention or be in a delayed intervention group (which also served as the control group). Findings from the study revealed that children participating in the intervention group showed greater gains in self-regulation over the school year than children participating in the control group (Schmitt et al., 2015). There were also a significant number of children who were dual language learners in the second study. Children who were dual language learners participating in the intervention experienced large gains in early math skills greater than those experienced by children who were dual language learners in the control group (also discussed in greater length in Chapter 5).

The findings from these studies are exciting because they provide evidence that circle time games can be used to improve self-regulation in preschool and into kindergarten. Especially exciting are the results showing that participating in the circle time games in the Kindergarten

Readiness Study led to academic gains over the preschool year and into kindergarten. This provides further evidence supporting the importance of self-regulation for children's academic achievement and school success. Importantly, none of the games used in either study included a focus on math or reading skills.

What makes the Kindergarten Readiness Study unique is how simple the intervention is—the games are easy to implement and require only a few materials, which are typically found in early childhood classrooms (e.g., construction paper). The games can be easily integrated into the preschool day, such as during circle time or music and movement. Although the games are simple, they increase in cognitive complexity over time and have been shown to lead to real and measurable growth in children's self-regulation and academic skills. These gains in self-regulation were measured by looking at children's gains on two direct measures of self-regulation—the Head-Toes-Knees-Shoulders task (HTKS) and the Dimensional Change Card Sorting task (the DCCS) (see Chapter 8 for more information on self-regulation assessment).

As we discussed in Chapter 3, best practices for promoting self-regulation include: modeling self-regulation by adults and peers, teaching self-regulation skills, increasing the complexity of children's self-regulation activities over time, providing children with opportunities to practice self-regulation across different contexts, and giving children supportive feedback to guide them toward pro-social and well-regulated behaviors and strategies.

The primary focus of the Kindergarten Readiness Study was directly teaching self-regulation skills and increasing the complexity of tasks and activities over time (although each of the other best practices was integrated to some degree). To ensure that children are learning not only self-regulation skills in the context of the games but also how to apply these skills across the contexts of their lives, games like those used in the Kindergarten Readiness Study should be used together with classroom practices that promote self-regulation growth for children throughout the rest of the school day (see Chapters 1–3 for specific strategies and ideas). If participating in self-regulation games during circle time twice per week over eight weeks can make a difference, think of what embedding self-regulation across the day could do!

● ● ● ● ●

Learning Checkpoint #1

1. Like any research study, the Kindergarten Readiness Study has strengths and limitations. What is one strength you noticed about the Kindergarten Readiness Study? What is one limitation or weakness?

As we mentioned earlier, although circle time lessons are important, what happens before and after circle time and how circle time is managed impact a child's ability to learn from the learning activities presented during circle time. In the next section, we share lessons learned from the Kindergarten Readiness Study by presenting "Ten Tips for a Well-Regulated Circle Time."

●●●●●

Ten Tips for a Well-Regulated Circle Time

1. *Set yourself up for success.* Circle time requires children to use regulatory skills that other parts of the preschool day do not. For example, during circle time, children are asked to sit still, pay attention, listen, and take turns in ways that are not required during less structured types of activities (e.g., free choice, centers, outdoor play). When setting up and structuring your circle time, think about the following:

   a. *Consider timing.* If circle time is your first activity of the day, children may be anxious to move their bodies. Include activities that allow them to be active and release energy before activities that require children to sit still. If circle time follows outside time, children may be more willing and able to sit down and pay attention to a quiet lesson, especially if a transition song or activity is used first to help children calm their bodies.

   b. *Provide children with a home base.* Have mats or carpet squares for children to sit on during circle time. Mats give children a designated seat and a "home base" to return to following activities that allow them to move around the circle time space (e.g., the sleeping game presented in Chapter 3). Many teachers use inexpensive cloth placemats or donated carpet samples.

   c. *Choose a quiet sign.* Choose a quiet sign to use when it is time to end an activity, calm down, or return to home base. Your quiet sign might simply be putting one hand up in the air, ringing a bell, or even singing a certain song.

2. *Create a circle time routine.* If you are not doing so already, consider adding a structure to your circle time. Many teachers find it helpful to think of circle time as a three-stage process, including a welcome and warm-up, lesson, and closing. Research shows that teachers with effective classroom management techniques (e.g., teachers who implement consistent and stable routines) promote children's self-regulation in the classroom (Rimm-Kaufman, Curby, Grimm, Nathanson, & Brock, 2009).

   a. *Circle time welcome.* Many teachers use a similar routine from day to day during the welcome/warm-up. For example, teachers may use the same greeting song (or rotate between a few greeting songs) to welcome children to the circle, followed by talking about the day of the week or the weather before proceeding to the lesson. If the lessons you plan for circle time typically require children to sit still, consider creating a welcome and warm-up routine that allows children to move their bodies first. Having the opportunity to release some energy (especially if circle time is at the beginning of the day) may improve children's abilities to focus and pay attention to the quieter components of circle time.

b. *Circle time lesson.* The lesson is at the heart of each circle time. Often, a lesson will correspond with a classroom theme (e.g., caterpillars and butterflies, five senses). Many of the activities presented at the end of each chapter in this book can be used as part of circle time lessons.

c. *Circle time closing.* The circle time closing typically includes a review of the topic discussed during the lesson and sharing what is happening next, followed by the teacher excusing children (individually or as a group) from the circle. Preparing children for the following activity can ease the transition from circle time by providing children who are waiting for their turn (perhaps to use the bathroom or to choose a center) with something to do while waiting. Consider the activity that follows circle time when choosing a closing activity. If circle time is followed by having children use the bathroom and wash their hands for snack, you may want to choose a closing activity that excuses one child at a time to prevent long lines in the bathroom.

3. *Choose activities that are developmentally appropriate for the children in your class and present activities in fun and engaging ways.* Be sure that the activities that you choose are appropriate for the children in your class based on their individual and collective abilities. Developmentally appropriate curricula integrate multiple domains of development and use many different approaches (including play, activities, and games) to promote learning (NAEYC, 2009). If the majority of children in your class seem bored or have difficulty paying attention and staying on task during circle time, this may be an indication that the activity is not developmentally appropriate and is either too challenging (leading to feelings of frustration) or not challenging enough (leading to feelings of boredom), or that the activity has lasted too long.

a. *Use emotional expression to promote engagement.* Your own emotional expression plays an important part in how children will respond to the activities you present. Have you ever attended a meeting or class where the teacher spoke with a monotone voice? How did students respond to the lesson? How did you respond to the lesson? Were you interested? Were you able to pay attention or did you end up daydreaming or even falling asleep? Showing enthusiasm through your facial expressions and voice can help children feel that same enthusiasm for learning. A high level of enthusiasm all the time, however, can also be overwhelming, so balancing enthusiasm with a range of emotional expressions is important. Use a quiet expression and voice when reading a calm book or introducing an activity that requires a low level of energy. Model the emotions of book characters in your own facial expression, body, and voice when you read a story.

4. *Model the behavior that you would like to see.* Children look to you to set an example for their behavior, and research shows that teachers need to demonstrate strong regulatory skills in order for children to properly learn these same skills (Jennings & Greenberg, 2009). If your circle time activity calls for quiet focus, express calm in your own body and voice so that children will follow suit. When challenging situations arise, such as a child showing a breakdown in self-regulation, it is important to model appropriate behavior then as well. For instance, if you are having a particularly stressful day and circle time feels out of hand, rather than yelling, "Shut up and sit down, all of you!" express yourself in the way you would like to see children express themselves when they are frustrated. Share your feelings, and use the same regulation skills that you would like to see in children. Remain calm and try saying, "Everyone please sit down. I am feeling very frustrated today because I feel like no one is listening to me." Not all children will respond to this approach (not all children respond to any approach), but all children will see the example that you set and your example will provide them with a model for positive and appropriate behavior that will help shape the choices they make in the future as they are developmentally able to do so.

5. *Provide opportunities for all children to participate and to feel successful.* Activities like those used in the Kindergarten Readiness Study allow children at different ages and developmental levels to participate successfully regardless of whether they can accurately follow all of the rules of the activity. Many of these games are cooperative in nature (e.g., Cooperative Freeze), and several offer opportunities for children to serve as leaders and models to their peers (e.g., Conductor, Drum Beats). By allowing children to participate at their own skill level (dancing to the music and freezing when it stops, even if they ignore the speed of the song), you can help children feel successful and capable. This approach facilitates participation and engagement, leading to a positive circle time experience. Ensuring

children's comfort and engagement in circle time and other learning activities will promote children's ability to follow increasingly complicated rules as children are developmentally ready.

6. *Allow children to participate in a way that is supportive of their personality and temperament.* Just like adults, children have varying levels of comfort in different situations. Some children will be excited to jump up and dance as soon as you turn on music. Others will feel more comfortable sitting on their carpet squares and watching their peers. Inviting and encouraging a child to try a new activity are part of the role of a supportive early childhood educator; however, allowing children to decline to participate in an activity if they are not comfortable doing so is also part of being a supportive educator. There are exceptions, of course, such as any activity related to a child's safety (e.g., participating in a fire drill). If a child is not actively participating in an activity (e.g., watching their peers hit the classroom drum rather than playing it themselves), it does not mean the child is not learning. There are many ways to engage in an activity (e.g., participating, watching, or leading), and offering children opportunities to engage in a way that matches their individual personality and temperament will help them feel comfortable and make the most of the learning experience.

7. *Work with colleagues to create a self-regulation support plan.* Carefully planning circle time and the transitions to and from circle time will help eliminate many of the challenges related to regulation that can arise during this time. Other challenges will arise, however, and having a plan in place to effectively support children who experience a breakdown in self-regulation in the middle of circle time will help avoid a situation that derails the entire class. The teacher leading circle time cannot effectively provide one-on-one attention to support a child who experiences difficulties during circle time. Having individual attention may be critical to providing a child with the external regulation help that the child needs to internally regulate during future circle times. Work together with your co-teacher(s) to come up with a plan to provide one-on-one support for children who need individual attention during circle time. This may mean having an assistant teacher available to sit next to a child who is likely to have difficulties or calling in additional support staff from the center.

8. *Have a backup plan.* As teachers, we have good days and bad days, great ideas and ideas that flop. In the event that a lesson "flops," materials that you need are unavailable for your lesson, or outdoor time needs to be brought indoors because of weather, have another activity ready to take its place. Many of the ideas presented throughout this book will work well as supplemental (or substitute) circle time activities and could be implemented with a moment's notice.

9. *Use every circle time as a learning experience for the children and you.* After each circle time, consider moments that went well and moments that did not. Take a few minutes to reflect on why these moments went well and what challenges you experienced, and brainstorm ways to extend the positive aspects of circle time or restructure those aspects that are challenging. Every day brings a new opportunity to evolve as an educator and try again.

10. *Have fun and maintain a sense of humor!* Teaching is hard work. As an early childhood educator, you are required to be engaged and involved every minute that you spend in the classroom. This can be emotionally exhausting. Additionally, the administrative work, child assessments, classroom planning and management, and other responsibilities of teaching can be overwhelming. Remember to take time to enjoy being with the children in your class. Studies have found significant links between positive student-teacher relationships and children's social skills (including self-regulation) and behavior in the classroom (Rimm-Kaufman et al., 2002; Rimm-Kaufman, La Paro, Downer, & Pianta, 2005). Taking the time to be present and enjoy yourself will remind you of why you went into this line of work, will help reduce your stress level, and will foster a positive relationship between you and the children in your classroom.

Reflect

After reading through the section on "Ten Tips for a Well-Regulated Circle Time," think about your own circle time routine. Which of these tips are you already integrating into your current classroom practices? Did you read any tips that you feel could help enhance your circle time?

Set a Goal

Choose at least two strategies presented in this chapter to enhance circle time in your classroom. After trying these strategies, reflect on how well they worked. What worked well? What challenges did you experience? What would you do differently next time?

●　●　●　●　●

Additional Resources

See Chapter 9 for additional resources related to the contents of this chapter, including Internet resources focusing on self-regulation activities and games and early childhood intervention programs targeting self-regulation.

● ● ● ● ●

References

Diamond, A., Barnett, W. S., Thomas, J., & Munro, S. (2007). Preschool program improves cognitive control. *Science, 318,* 1387–1388.

Jennings, P. A., & Greenberg, M. T. (2009). The prosocial classroom: Teacher social and emotional competence in relation to student and classroom outcomes. *Review of Educational Research, 79*(1), 491–525.

National Association for the Education of Young Children. (2009). *NAEYC position statement: Developmentally appropriate practice in early childhood programs serving children from birth through age 8.* Retrieved January 12, 2012, from www.naeyc.org/files/naeyc/file/positions/PSDAP.pdf

Pears, K. C., Fisher, P. A., Bruce, J., Kim, H. K., & Yoerger, K. (2010). Early elementary school adjustment of maltreated children in foster care: The roles of inhibitory control and caregiver involvement. *Child Development, 81*(5), 1550–1564. doi:10.1111/j.1467–8624.2010.01491.x

Raver, C. C., Jones, S. M., Li-Grining, C., Zhai, F., Bub, K., & Pressler, E. (2011). CSRP's impact on low-income preschoolers' preacademic skills: Self-regulation as a mediating mechanism. *Child Development, 82*(1), 362–378. doi:10.1111/j.1467–8624.2010.01561.x

Rimm-Kaufman, S. E., Curby, T. W., Grimm, K. J., Nathanson, L., & Brock, L. L. (2009). The contribution of children's self-regulation and classroom quality to children's adaptive behaviors in the kindergarten classroom. *Developmental Psychology, 45*(4), 958–972.

Rimm-Kaufman, S. E., Early, D. M., Cox, M. J., Saluja, G., Pianta, R. C., Bradley, R. H., & Payne, C. (2002). Early behavioral attributes and teachers' sensitivity as predictors of competent behavior in the kindergarten classroom. *Journal of Applied Developmental Psychology, 23*(4), 451.

Rimm-Kaufman, S. E., La Paro, K. M., Downer, J. T., & Pianta, R. C. (2005). The contribution of classroom setting and quality of instruction to children's behavior in kindergarten classrooms. *Elementary School Journal, 105*(4), 377–394.

Rivers, S. E., Tominey, S., O' Bryon, E., & Brackett, M. (2013). Developing emotional skills in early childhood settings using Preschool RULER. *Psychology of Education Review, 37,* 20–25.

Schmitt, S. A., McClelland, M. M., Tominey, S. L., & Acock, A. C. (2015). Strengthening school readiness for Head Start children: Evaluation of a self-regulation intervention. *Early Childhood Research Quarterly, 30,* 20–31.

Tominey, S. L., & McClelland, M. M. (2011). Red light, purple light: Findings from a randomized trial using circle time games to improve behavioral self-regulation in preschool. *Early Education and Development, 22*(3), 489–519.

Tominey, S., & McClelland, M. M. (2013). Quantitative and qualitative factors related to the effectiveness of a preschool behavioral regulation intervention. *National Head Start Association Dialog, 16*(3), 21–44.

ACTIVITY BREAK #2: SUPPORTING CIRCLE TIME TRANSITIONS THROUGH SELF-REGULATION

The activities in this section are intended to help support the transitions in and out of circle time. Some of these activities can also be used to help support transitions at other times throughout the day, including waiting in line to use the bathroom, sitting at the lunch/ snack table, and walking down the hallway.

"Do You Know My Friends?"

(Circle time welcome)

> To the tune of: "The Muffin Man"
> Do you know my friend *Lily*?
> My friend *Aidan*?
> My friend *Matilda*?
> Do you know my friend *Julian*?

They are at school today.

Procedure: Sing and repeat this song as you name all of the children and teachers in the circle. You can also add another level of complexity to the song by having children pass an item (e.g., ball, baton, stuffed animal) around the circle as their name is sung.

Funny Faces Song

(Circle time, small group, transitions)

> To the tune of: "Mary Had a Little Lamb"
> *Ethan* makes a funny face, funny face, funny face.
> *Ethan* makes a funny face. Watch and copy him.

Procedure: Start by modeling the game for the children in your class by inserting your name in the song and making a funny face (e.g., "Ms. Emily makes a funny face."). Sing the song together, and make a funny face at the end of the verse. Ask children to copy the face you are making. Ask if anyone else would like a turn to make a funny face, and choose one child at a time to demonstrate his or her own funny face as you sing the song together. See Figure 4.1 for an image of a child singing the Funny Faces song.

Skill development: This activity helps children practice attentional flexibility by encouraging them to turn their attention to a classmate

Figure 4.1 A Child Singing the Funny Faces Song.
Photo by Shauna Tominey.

and switch that attention with each verse of the song. Children are often accustomed to focusing on the teacher and can find it challenging to switch their focus from teachers to peers.

Funny Faces Song Variation

Procedure: Rather than making "funny" faces, have children make various feeling faces. For example, sing, "Rachel makes a sad face, sad face, sad face." Have children look at Rachel, copy her face, and discuss what makes a face a sad face ("What are our mouths doing? What about our eyebrows?"). Repeat the song, allowing additional children to have a turn making a range of feeling faces (e.g., angry face, sad/disappointed face, scared face, surprised face).

Skill development: Helping children recognize emotional expressions in others lays a foundation for emotion regulation. Understanding the effect our actions can have on others is often reflected in the face of a classmate who is smiling ("I liked what you did!") or frowning ("I did not like that."). Drawing children's attention to this fact will help them practice emotion recognition and support their perspective-taking abilities.

Getting to Know You

(Circle time welcome, transitions)

Materials: None

Procedure: Tell children that you are going to play a game to learn more about one another. Ask children to hold two thumbs up for things that they like and two thumbs down for things that they do not like. Ask children a series of questions: "Who likes strawberries?" "Who likes broccoli?" Help children get to know one another better and to get to know you by pointing out similarities and differences in likes and dislikes (e.g., "It looks like I am the only one who likes green beans!"). Change the nature of the questions that you ask to reflect things that children have done or places children have been (e.g., "Who has flown in an airplane?" "Who has been to the library before?"). Make the game more complicated by asking children to perform different actions. For example, ask children to put their hands on their head if they have done something and put their hands in their lap if they have not.

Skill development: In this activity, children are practicing self-regulation by attending to each question that is asked and using their memory to remember and follow through with instructions (e.g., touch your nose if you . . .). Children are also building social relationships through developing awareness of others around them and identifying similarities and differences between themselves and their peers.

If You're Wearing Blue Today

(Circle time closing, transitions)

To the tune of: "If You're Happy and You Know It"
If you're *wearing blue today, wash your hands.*
If you're *wearing blue today, wash your hands.*
If you're *wearing blue today,* if you're *wearing blue today.*
If you're *wearing blue today, wash your hands!*

Procedure: Sing this song to excuse small groups of children from the circle at one time. Substitute "If you're wearing blue today" with other descriptive words (e.g., "If you have long hair today" or "If you are four years old today"). Substitute "wash your hands" with the next activity (e.g., "find your coat" or "choose a center").

Jack Be Nimble

(Circle time closing, transitions)

> *Jack* be nimble, *Jack* be quick,
> *Jack* jump over the candlestick!

Materials: Rectangular block (or another object to represent a candlestick)

Procedure: This chant can be used to excuse one child at a time from the circle. Place the "candlestick" in the center of the circle. Replace Jack's name in the chant with the name of a child in the circle. When the child's name is called, he or she can stand up, jump over the candlestick, and leave the circle to start the next activity (e.g., washing hands for snack, choosing a center activity).

Let's See Who's at School Today

(Circle time welcome)

> To the tune of: "Old MacDonald Had a Farm"
> Let's see who's at school today.
> E – I – E – I – O.
> Friends who came to learn and play.
> E – I – E – I – O.
> Is everybody here? Let's play a game.
> Point to a friend and say their name.
> Let's see who's at school today.
> E – I – E – I – O.

Procedure: After singing the song, lead children in pointing their fingers to each child and teacher in the circle and reciting each of their names (e.g., "Jim is here. Ethan is here. Cassie is here. McKayla is here."). After naming all children and teachers in the circle, ask the children, "Who is missing today?" Allow children time to think about and name the children who are absent.

Let's Wave Our Hands and Sing Hello

(Circle time welcome)

> To the tune of: "Wheels on the Bus"
> Let's *wave our hands* and sing hello.
> Sing hello. Sing hello.
> Let's *wave our hands* and sing hello.
> We're at school today.

Procedure: Encourage children to wave their hands while singing the song. Sing the song multiple times, replacing "wave our hands" with other actions (e.g., stomp our feet, wiggle our arms, stick out our tongues). Actions can be chosen that support your classroom theme. For example, if your weekly theme is "Feelings," actions can include "make a happy face," "stomp your feet like you're angry," or "act surprised."

Pass the Ball Around the Room

(Circle time welcome)

> To the tune of: "London Bridge"
> Pass the ball around the room.
> Taking turns with every friend.
> Say your name and pass the ball
> And watch it come around again.

Procedure: Sing the song, and then have each child say his or her own name as he or she passes the ball around the room. Children who are extremely shy may not want to say their name out loud. Encourage them to try, but if they do not want to, say their name for them or along with them and then pass the ball to the next child.

Skill development: In this activity, children practice attentional flexibility by attending to the words of the song (and remembering the words to sing along). They are also given the opportunity to practice additional social skills (making eye contact with friends, saying their own name) and gross motor skills (passing the ball to a friend).

There Was a Boy/Girl Who Came to School

(Circle time closing)

> To the tune of: "Bingo"
> There was a *boy* who came to school and *Jacob* was his name-o.
> *Stomp and clap your hands.*
> *Stomp and clap your hands.*
> *Stomp and clap your hands.*
> And now go *wash your hands!*

Procedure: This is another song that can be used to excuse children one at a time from the circle while keeping other children actively engaged. Substitute "Stomp and clap your hands" with different actions (e.g., "Stand and shake your head").

There Was a Boy/Girl Who Came to School Variation #1

This song can also be used as a circle time welcome song. If there are too many children in your class to introduce each individually, you can introduce several children with each verse of the song:

There were three friends who came to school
Lia, Cameron, and Miguel are their names-o!
Wave your arms and shake your head.
Wave your arms and shake your head.
Wave your arms and shake your head.
We're all at school today-o!

5

●●●●●

Self-Regulation and Curriculum Areas
Literacy and Math

Ms. Joanne sat down to work on her lesson plans for the following week. She wanted to continue exploring the "doctor's office" theme, which had emerged after one child in her class brought in a picture from a recent checkup. She laid out her state's early learning standards and the Head Start standards and started thinking about ways in which she could integrate various curriculum areas into doctor's office-focused activities. On Monday, she planned to set up the dramatic play area as a doctor's office, complete with dress-up clothes and doctor kits to embed social and emotional skills into an exploration of the theme. At morning meeting, she would extend their social and emotional learning by reading a story about a character who was feeling afraid to go to the doctor and talk with children about why going to the doctor is important (e.g., to help make sure our bodies are healthy) and what they could do or say to themselves if they were feeling nervous about going to the doctor to help themselves feel brave. To embed literacy, she planned to have children practice writing letters by asking them to help make signs to post around the dramatic play area (e.g., "Doctor's Office," "scale," "wait here"). At small group time, they would practice early math and critical thinking skills by playing a game ("What's Missing?") using items from a toy doctor's kit.

In the same way that early childhood educators like Ms. Joanne embed early learning areas into classroom themes and lesson planning, self-regulation can be embedded as well. Not only can self-regulation be embedded into classroom management (as we shared in Chapter 3) or circle time (Chapter 4), but also it can be embedded into activities focused on promoting early academic skills. Over a decade of research has demonstrated that self-regulation is important for children's academic success in both reading and math. This is not surprising because there is significant evidence showing that having strong self-regulation helps children take advantage of learning activities. In this chapter, we provide an overview of early academic skills with an emphasis on pre-reading and early math skills. We share research on the connections between self-regulation and early academic skills and share specific ways that self-regulation can be embedded into activities promoting academic success.

● ● ● ● ●

Laying the Foundation for Early Academic Success With Self-Regulation

In preschool, numerous aspects of self-regulation, such as being able to focus, pay attention, and remember and follow directions, have been shown to help children benefit from early learning activities. A substantial body of research shows that self-regulation is important for children's reading achievement as early as preschool. Research shows that the relationship between preschool self-regulation and reading persists throughout elementary school and high school (Best, Miller, & Naglieri, 2011; McClelland, Acock, & Morrison, 2006; McClelland, Acock, Piccinin, Rhea, & Stallings, 2013). Studies have also shown significant connections between self-regulation and early literacy skills. For example, studies have shown that children's self-regulation in preschool relates to aspects of children's emergent literacy, such as oral language and phonological awareness (Boss, 2014; Connor et al., 2010; McClelland et al., 2007, 2013; Schmitt, Pentimonti, & Justice, 2012; Skibbe, Phillips, Day, Brophy-Herb, & Connor, 2012). As children get older, self-regulation has also been significantly related to more advanced literacy skills, such as children's understanding of writing and composition (Boss, 2014).

Although self-regulation has been consistently related to many different academic skills, it is often found to be most strongly related to early math skills (Bull, Espy, & Wiebe, 2008; Cameron Ponitz, McClelland, Matthews, & Morrison, 2009; Clark, Pritchard, & Woodward, 2010). Like self-regulation, children's early math skills have been identified as an important predictor of later academic achievement (Claessens, Duncan, & Engel, 2009; Clements & Sarama, 2009; Duncan et al., 2007; Sarama & Clements, 2009). Research suggests that early self-regulation is closely related to mathematical thinking skills as these skills tap similar areas of the brain, indicating they may require many of the same underlying processes (Diamond & Lee, 2011; Dowsett & Livesey, 2000).

Pre-Reading Skills in Preschool

The preschool years are an important period for the development of pre-reading and emergent literacy skills (e.g., Whitehurst & Lonigan,

1998). Children are often told that they will learn to read once they go to kindergarten, but there are many skills that they can develop in preschool that lay the foundation for later reading abilities. Instead of seeing reading as a skill that develops once children get to formal schooling (kindergarten in the U.S.), recent perspectives recognize that emergent literacy and pre-reading skills begin to develop early and many of these skills are viewed as necessary precursors to reading and writing (Lonigan, Burgess, & Anthony, 2000).

In preschool, there are three components of emergent literacy that form the foundation for reading skills. These components can be tied to standards, such as the Common Core State Standards (CCSS, 2002), and include oral language, phonological awareness, and print knowledge. Oral language skills refer to children's knowledge of words and word order, vocabulary skills, and the rules of grammar (Storch & Whitehurst, 2002). Phonological awareness includes using matching, blending, or word deletion to identify and manipulate language (Wagner & Torgesen, 1987). Print knowledge refers to the basic conventions of print, such as how to hold and use books (e.g., turning pages in the proper direction), the directionality of print (reading from left to right), and letter names and sounds (Whitehurst & Lonigan, 1998).

Early Math Skills in Preschool

Like reading skills, the development of mathematical skills emerges during early childhood, long before formal schooling (i.e., kindergarten) starts (Ginsberg & Pappas, 2004; Swanson, 2006). During the preschool years, children develop many aspects of early mathematical thinking, including learning about numbers, quantitative reasoning (e.g., understanding that five is greater than four and size comparisons), addition and subtraction, and visual-spatial reasoning (e.g., learning about shape, size, location) (De Feyter & Winsler, 2009). Research has documented that even by preschool, there are substantial differences between children in early math abilities (Jordan, Kaplan, Ramineni, & Locuniak, 2009). This is important because these early math skills predict children's math achievement throughout the elementary years (Duncan et al., 2007; National Center on Immigrant Integration and Policy, 2010). Children who lag behind their peers in early math are likely to continue struggling with these skills. Not only do early math skills predict later math skills, but also they predict children's abilities in other areas. For example, aspects of early mathematical thinking, including children's quantitative reasoning (e.g., understanding relative size comparisons), counting and cardinality (e.g., one-to-one correspondence, counting out a sequence verbally, and comparing numbers), the meaning of numbers, number relationships, and mathematical operations (e.g., simple adding and subtracting), predict elementary math and reading achievement (Cosden, Zimmer, Reyes, & Gutierrez, 1995; Duncan et al., 2007; National Center on Immigrant Integration and Policy, 2010). Children's geometric ability to identify, describe, analyze, compare, and create shapes is also a key aspect of early mathematical thinking and important for achievement (Starkey, Klein, & Wakeley, 2004). The importance of early math skills has been recognized in the Kindergarten Common Core State Standards (Common Core State Standards Initiative, 2002, para. 1), which states that "more learning time in Kindergarten should be devoted to number than to other topics." Despite this awareness of the importance of early math skills, children's math scores in the U.S. are substantially lower than those in most other countries (Clements & Sarama, 2009; Hanushek, Peterson, & Woessmann, 2010; Sarama & Clements, 2009).

Promoting Early Academic Skills

Importantly, pre-reading skills and early math skills are malleable—they can be taught, practiced, and improved. As might be expected, promoting early literacy and math skills is more effective when these academic skills are embedded into the classroom through engaging activities or games rather than as separate literacy or math instruction (e.g., flash cards) (Arnold, Fisher, Doctoroff, & Dobbs, 2002; Casey, Kersh, & Young, 2004; Hong, 1996; Justice & Pullen, 2003; Seo & Ginsberg, 2004). For example, activities that have been shown to promote emergent literacy skills and pre-reading skills include dialogic book reading (e.g. where the child becomes an active participant in telling the story and the adult listens, questions, and provides an audience for the child), literacy-enriched play interventions (i.e., literacy props and materials embedded into familiar and meaningful classroom-based activities), and teacher-led activities (i.e., teachers engage children in developmentally sequenced literacy games that include rhyming, alphabet and sound identification, and phoneme blending and segmenting; Justice & Pullen, 2003).

For math, games such as the "Great Race" (Siegler & Ramani, 2008), a game that includes sequentially numbered spaces to help young children learn about the number line and the relative magnitude of numbers, and activities that involve books, music, and interactive games (Arnold et al., 2002) have led to strong improvements in children's early math skills. Other programs, such as Building Blocks, have also been shown to improve children's math, language, and executive function skills by more intentional focus on math activities in preschool classrooms (Clements & Sarama, 2007). Together, this research suggests that aspects of emergent literacy and mathematical thinking during the preschool years are important components of school readiness interventions. In addition, literacy and math integrated with other intervention components (e.g., self-regulation games) may be an effective alternative to traditional academic instruction. In fact, some promising research has shown that interventions focusing on self-regulation can be effective ways to increase these skills in young children.

• • • • •

Learning Checkpoint #1

1. At your center, how strongly are academic skills emphasized in relation to social skills like self-regulation? In other words, is one set of skills prioritized over the other or is equal weight placed on both sets of skills?

Kindergarten Readiness Study and Links to Academic Achievement

As we shared in Chapter 4, our research on the Kindergarten Readiness Study suggests that practicing self-regulation can have important payoffs for children's emergent literacy and math skills. In our pilot test with 65 children, children randomly assigned to the intervention group exhibited significant gains in early literacy compared to children in the control group, even though none of the games included literacy components. These results suggest that gains in self-regulation impacted early academic skills. In another test of the Kindergarten Readiness Study with 279 children from low-income families, children participating in the intervention group who were dual language learners showed significant gains in early math skills in comparison to children in the control group (Schmitt, McClelland, Tominey, & Acock, 2015). In fact, these children made a 23-point gain, which translated to a one-year math gain in six months! Children who were dual language learners in the intervention group even made bigger gains in math compared to English speakers who participated in the intervention (an 11-point gain in math). Although our circle time games did not specifically focus on math concepts, promoting children's self-regulation resulted in significant math gains. These results support the important links between early self-regulation and math skills. They also suggest that promoting math and self-regulation can have beneficial effects on school readiness for all children, but especially those who are experiencing risk early in life (e.g., living in poverty). In addition, using games that include both self-regulation and academic components and that can be effectively integrated into classroom curricula may have the greatest effect on strengthening school readiness for children.

Other research has taken the circle time games from the Kindergarten Readiness Study and incorporated them into a summer program for children from disadvantaged backgrounds prior to entering kindergarten. Teachers administered the intervention games every day over three weeks to about 1,450 children. In the most recent evaluation, children participating in the circle time games demonstrated significant and substantial gains in self-regulation and academic achievement from the beginning of summer to the fall of kindergarten. By the end of fall, children in the summer program had made gains in self-regulation and math that were the equivalent of about 12 months of normal development in just four months. Moreover, by the end of fall, children receiving the intervention games had also improved in early literacy skills equivalent to more than six months of typical development in just four months.

Taken together, the research linking self-regulation and early academic skills is compelling! Having strong self-regulation gives children the skills they need to benefit from early learning activities, helping children build a strong foundation for success in literacy and math. If children struggle with self-regulation in preschool, they are likely to fall behind their peers academically. Moreover, reading and math skills are cumulative. If children do not have the self-regulation they need to build a strong foundation in these skills early, they are likely to experience achievement gaps. Alarmingly, research shows that achievement gaps tend to widen over time—that it becomes more and more challenging to catch up as children fall farther and farther behind (McClelland et al., 2006).

It is also important to point out that the relationship between self-regulation skills and early academic skills is not entirely clear. Although strong evidence suggests that self-regulation is critical for children to be able to learn, there is debate around whether self-regulation needs to be developed first in order for children to learn academic skills or if these skills develop hand in hand. The close connections between self-regulation and early academic achievement suggest that promoting both skills together could be especially effective in young children. In preschool, educators can use fun and engaging games and activities to help children practice and improve self-regulation as well as early academic skills. Embedding self-regulation into early academic areas can help educators create activities that are developmentally appropriate and fun, meeting the interests and developmental levels of children in diverse classes. In the next section, we provide specific games and activity ideas for embedding self-regulation into pre-reading and early math skill development.

Reflect

What do you do to promote early literacy and math skills in fun and engaging ways with the children in your class? Which activities that you use do children like the most? Why do you think that is?

Set a Goal

Choose at least two activities from "Activity Break #3: Self-Regulation Games Promoting Literacy and Math" to try in your own classroom. After integrating these activities in your own lesson plans, reflect on how well they worked. What did children like about the activities you chose? Were there any challenges? How would you modify these activities in the future?

● ● ● ● ●

Additional Resources

See Chapter 9 for additional resources related to the contents of this chapter, including Internet resources focusing on early literacy and math.

● ● ● ● ●

References

Arnold, D. H., Fisher, P. H., Doctoroff, G. L., & Dobbs, J. (2002). Accelerating math development in Head Start classrooms. *Journal of Educational Psychology, 94*(4), 762–770.

Best, J. R., Miller, P. H., & Naglieri, J. A. (2011). Relations between executive function and academic achievement from ages 5 to 17 in a large, representative national sample. *Learning and Individual Differences, 21*(4), 327–336. doi:10.1016/j.lindif.2011.01.007

Boss, E. (2014). *The relation between self-regulation skills and emergent and early writing in preschool and kindergarten children* (Unpublished thesis). University of Pittsburgh, PA. Retrieved from http://d-scholarship.pitt.edu/21155

Bull, R., Espy, K. A., & Wiebe, S. A. (2008). Short-term memory, working memory, and executive functioning in preschoolers: Longitudinal predictors of mathematical achievement at age 7 years. *Developmental Neuropsychology, 33*(3), 205–228. doi:10.1080/87565640801982312

Cameron Ponitz, C. E., McClelland, M. M., Matthews, J. M., & Morrison, F. J. (2009). A structured observation of behavioral self-regulation and its contribution to kindergarten outcomes. *Developmental Psychology, 45*(3), 605–619. doi:10.1037/a0015365

Casey, B., Kersh, J. E., & Young, J. M. (2004). Storytelling sagas: An effective medium for teaching early childhood mathematics. *Early Childhood Research Quarterly, 19*, 167–172.

Claessens, A., Duncan, G., & Engel, M. (2009). Kindergarten skills and fifth-grade achievement: Evidence from the ECLS-K. *Economics of Education Review, 28*(4), 415–427. doi:10.1016/j.econedurev.2008.09.003

Clark, C. A. C., Pritchard, V. E., & Woodward, L. J. (2010). Preschool executive functioning abilities predict early mathematics achievement. *Developmental Psychology, 46*(5), 1176–1191. doi:10.1037/a0019672

Clements, D. H., & Sarama, J. (2007). Effects of a preschool mathematics curriculum: Summative research on the Building Blocks project. *Journal for Research in Mathematics Education, 38*(2), 136–163.

Clements, D. H., & Sarama, J. (2009). *Learning and teaching early math: The Learning Trajectories Approach.* New York, NY: Routledge.

Common Core State Standards Initiative. (2002). Mathematics: Kindergarten. Retrieved August 1, 2013, from www.corestandards.org/Math/Content/K/introduction

Connor, C. M., Ponitz, C. C., Phillips, B. M., Travis, Q. M., Glasney, S., & Morrison, F. J. (2010). First graders' literacy and self-regulation gains: The effect of individualizing student instruction. *Journal of School Psychology, 48,* 433–455. doi:10.1016/j.jsp.2010.06.003

Cosden, M., Zimmer, J., Reyes, C., & Gutierrez, M. R. (1995). Kindergarten practices and first-grade achievement for Latino Spanish-speaking, Latino English-speaking, and Anglo students. *Journal of School Psychology, 33*(2), 123–141. doi:10.1002/icd.469

De Feyter, J. J., & Winsler, A. (2009). The early developmental competencies and school readiness of low-income, immigrant children: Influences of generation race/ethnicity, and national origins. *Early Childhood Research Quarterly, 24,* 411–431.

Diamond, A., & Lee, K. (2011). Interventions shown to aid executive function development in children 4 to 12 years old. *Science, 333*(6045), 959–964. doi:10.1126/science.1204529

Dowsett, S. M., & Livesey, D. J. (2000). The development of inhibitory control in preschool children: Effects of "executive skills" training. *Developmental Psychobiology, 36*(2), 161–174.

Duncan, G. J., Dowsett, C. J., Claessens, A., Magnuson, K., Huston, A. C., Klebanov, P., . . . Japel, C. (2007). School readiness and later achievement. *Developmental Psychology, 43*(6), 1428–1446. doi:10.1037/0012–1649.43.6.1428

Ginsberg, H. P., & Pappas, S. (2004). SES, ethnic, and gender differences in young children's informal addition and subtraction: A clinical interview investigation. *Applied Developmental Psychology, 25,* 171–192.

Hanushek, E. A., Peterson, P. E., & Woessmann, L. (2010). *U.S. math performance in global perspective.* Boston, MA: Harvard University, Harvard Kennedy School of Government.

Hong, H. (1996). Effects of mathematics learning through children's literature on math achievement and dispositional outcomes. *Early Childhood Research Quality, 11*(4), 477–494.

Jordan, N. C., Kaplan, D., Ramineni, C., & Locuniak, M. N. (2009). Early math matters: Kindergarten number competence and later mathematics outcomes. *Developmental Psychology, 45*(3), 850–867. doi:10.1037/a0014939

Justice, L. M., & Pullen, P. C. (2003). Promising interventions for promoting emergent literacy skills: Three evidence-based approaches. *Topics in Early Childhood Special Education, 23*(3), 99–113.

Lonigan, C. J., Burgess, S., & Anthony, J. (2000). Development of emergent literacy and early reading skills in preschool children: Evidence from a latent variable longitudinal study. *Developmental Psychology, 36*(5), 596–613.

McClelland, M. M., Acock, A. C., & Morrison, F. J. (2006). The impact of kindergarten learning-related skills on academic trajectories at the end of elementary school. *Early Childhood Research Quarterly, 21,* 471–490. doi:10.1016/j.ecresq.2006.09.003

McClelland, M. M., Acock, A. C., Piccinin, A., Rhea, S. A., & Stallings, M. C. (2013). Relations between preschool attention span-persistence and age 25 educational outcomes. *Early Childhood Research Quarterly, 28*(2), 314–324. doi:10.1016/j.ecresq.2012.07.008

McClelland, M. M., Cameron, C. E., Connor, C. M., Farris, C. L., Jewkes, A. M., & Morrison, F. J. (2007). Links between behavioral regulation and preschoolers' literacy, vocabulary and math skills. *Developmental Psychology, 43*(4), 947–959. doi:10.1037/0012–1649.43.4.947

National Center on Immigrant Integration and Policy. (2010). *Top languages spoken by English Language Learners nationally and by state.* www.migrationinformation.org/ellinfo/FactSheet_ELL3.pdf

Sarama, J., & Clements, D. H. (2009). *Early childhood mathematics education research: Learning trajectories for young children.* New York, NY: Routledge.

Schmitt, M. B., Pentimonti, J. M., & Justice, L. M. (2012). Teacher–child relationships, behavior regulation, and language gain among at-risk preschoolers. *Journal of School Psychology, 50*(5), 681–699.

Schmitt, S. A., McClelland, M. M., Tominey, S. L., & Acock, A. C. (2015). Strengthening school readiness for Head Start children: Evaluation of a self-regulation intervention. *Early Childhood Research Quarterly, 30*, 20–31.

Seo, K.-H., & Ginsberg, H. P. (2004). What is developmentally appropriate in early childhood mathematics education?: Lessons from new research. In D. H. Clements, J. Sarama, & A.-M. DiBiase (Eds.), *Engaging young children in mathematics: Standards for early childhood mathematics education* (pp. 91–104). Hillsdale, NJ: Erlbaum.

Siegler, R. S., & Ramani, G. B. (2008). Playing linear numerical board games promotes low-income children's numerical development. *Developmental Science, 11*(5), 655–661.

Skibbe, L. E., Phillips, B. M., Day, S. L., Brophy-Herb, H. E., & Connor, C. M. (2012). Children's early literacy growth in relation to classmates' self-regulation. *Journal of Educational Psychology, 104*(3), 541–553. doi:10.1037/a0029153

Starkey, P., Klein, A., & Wakeley, A. (2004). Enhancing young children's mathematical knowledge through a pre-kindergarten mathematics intervention. *Early Childhood Research Quarterly, 19*, 99–120.

Storch, S. A., & Whitehurst, G. J. (2002). Oral language and code-related precursors to reading: Evidence from a longitudinal structural model. *Developmental Psychology, 38*(6), 934–947. doi:10.1037/0012-1649.38.6.934

Swanson, H. L. (2006). Cognitive processes that underlie mathematical precociousness in young children. *Journal of Experimental Child Psychology, 93*(3), 187–284.

Wagner, R. K., & Torgesen, J. K. (1987). The nature of phonological processing and its causal role in the acquisition of reading skills. *Psychological Bulletin, 101*(2), 192–212. doi:10.1037/0033–2909.101.2.192

Whitehurst, G. J., & Lonigan, C. J. (1998). Child development and emergent literacy. *Child Development, 69*(3), 848–872.

ACTIVITY BREAK #3: SELF-REGULATION GAMES PROMOTING LITERACY AND MATH

Activities Using Self-Regulation to Promote Literacy Skills

ABCs—loud and soft

(Circle time, small group, or transition activity)

Materials: wooden dowel, wooden spoon, or baton (optional)

Procedure: Sing the Alphabet Song (the "ABCs") together. Now sing the song again, but this time act as a conductor and wave your arms (or a baton) as you sing. Have children sing loudly when you wave your arms up high and softly in a whisper when you wave your arms down low. To increase the complexity of this game, ask children to alternate between speaking and whispering with each letter.

Skill development: This activity requires children to demonstrate inhibitory control by making alternating loud and soft sounds and reinforcing their knowledge of the alphabet.

Initial consonant Simon Says

(Circle time, small group, or transition activity)

Materials: none

Procedure: This game can be played with individual children or in small or large groups. Help children practice learning initial consonant sounds by asking children to touch their head when you say a word that starts with an "H," touch their toes when you say a word that starts with a "T," and touch their nose if you say a word that starts with a different letter. As children become familiar with the game, use different body parts to represent words that start with different letters.

Skill development: This game requires children to pay attention and remember multi-step directions while learning to recognize letter sounds.

I spy something that starts with "A"

(Circle time, small group, or transition activity)

Materials:

■ Notecards with individual letters written on them.

Procedure: Show children the letter on the card (this example uses the letter A). Tell them, "I spy many things that begin with the letter A!" and ask them to point to items in the classroom that start with A. Together, look at each of the items that children point to ("It looks like Johnny found an apple! Caroline found a picture of an ant!"). As children become familiar with each letter over time, make the game more complicated by showing the card, but not reading the letter aloud ("I see many things that begin with this letter.").

Skill development: In this game, children are encouraged to pay attention to and follow through with the instructions while building letter recognition skills and applying these skills to their own understanding of letter sounds and initial consonants of items around the classroom.

Rhyme time

(Circle time, small group, or transition activity)

Materials: none

Procedure: Explain to children that you are going to play a rhyming game where you will say some words. Ask children to perform a certain action (e.g., nodding their head or putting their thumbs up) if the words rhyme and a different action if the words do not rhyme (e.g., shaking their head or putting their thumbs down). Say two or three words rhyming words in a row with the last word varying in whether it rhymes with the others (e.g., "cat, hat, sat, rat!" Did that rhyme? How about this one? "dog, hog, log, squirrel."). Allow children to have a turn and watch their classmates respond to their rhymes or non-rhymes.

Skill development: This activity emphasizes children's ability to pay attention, both to the teacher and to their peers. Children will also develop their attention to whether words rhyme and learn to produce and identify rhymes themselves.

Activities Using Self-Regulation to Promote Math Skills

Counting by twos

(Circle time, small group, or transition activity)

Materials: none

Procedure: Count together from 1 to 10 (or from 1 to 20). Now ask children to count together again, but this times alternate between saying numbers loudly and softly: one—TWO—three—FOUR—five—SIX—seven—EIGHT—nine—TEN. Practice this a few times on different days until children become comfortable with the pattern, and then encourage children to become even quieter on the soft numbers. Finally, have children say the quiet numbers in their heads and the loud numbers aloud. Children will be counting by twos!

Skill development: This game helps children develop counting skills while practicing attention, working memory, and inhibitory control.

Matching freeze game (colors, numbers, shapes, letters)

(Circle time, gross motor activity, or music and movement)

Materials:

- CD and CD player
- Construction paper cut into three different shapes (four each—e.g., four triangles, four squares, and four circles)
- Masking tape.

Procedure: Prior to playing this game, use the masking tape to secure three of each of the construction paper shapes to the ground around the circle time or gross motor area. Alternately, shapes can be taped to the walls. Keep one of each shape aside. Similar to Freeze Dancing (see Chapter 6), ask children to dance when the music plays and freeze when the music stops. Add a level of complexity to the game by holding up a shape when the music stops and asking children to find and stand on or point to a shape that matches your shape. You can make the game more complicated by saying the name of the shape instead of holding up a model (e.g., "Find a triangle!" "Find an oval!"). Alternately, you can focus on the number of sides on a shape (e.g., "Find a shape with three sides"), colors (e.g., "Find a red circle"), or add pictures or letters to the shapes (e.g., "Find a shape with the letter A").

Skill development: In this game children are practicing attentional flexibility by switching their focus from one task to another (dancing and freezing to finding a shape). Children develop their working memory skills by attending to and remembering fairly complex sets of instructions. They also practice inhibitory control in a number of ways, including through starting and stopping to music and looking to a teacher to provide visual or aural clues before finding a shape.

Number hop

(Circle time, gross motor activity)

Materials:

■ Notecards with individual numbers written on them.

Procedure: Choose an action (e.g., jumping up and down, clapping hands) or ask for an idea for an action from children in your class. Hold up a number card, read the number, and have children perform the action that number of times (e.g., jump six times). After rotating through a few number cards, choose (or ask a child to choose) a new action.

Skill development: Children are encouraged to pay attention to and remember the chosen action. They are also practicing number recognition, counting, and inhibitory control by performing the action the number of times written on the card.

What's missing?

(Small group or circle time)

Materials:

■ 3–8 items from around the classroom (items can all be within a classroom theme or independent of one another)
■ Towel, blanket, or large piece of cloth.

Procedure: Lay the items down on a tabletop or on the floor where children can see them clearly. Tell children the names of each item and describe any new item that children may not have seen before. Have children say the names of the items aloud together as you point to each one. Cover the items with the towel or blanket. Reach your hand under the towel, and remove one of the items so that the children cannot see which item was removed. Lift off the towel and ask children to figure out what is missing. Once children identify the missing item, put the item back and play the game again. Start with a small number of items (three or four) when introducing this game to your class to help support all children's ability to participate. To make the game more challenging, add additional items or move the items around with each new turn.

Skill development: This activity emphasizes children's working memory skills. It also embeds attention, vocabulary development (children learning the names of potentially new items), and deductive reasoning skills.

6

●●●●●

Integrating Self-Regulation Into Outdoor and Gross Motor Play

Monique looked around the playground. Wood chips, cement, and not much else. In fact, she didn't even like calling it a playground. It was no wonder children in her class asked if they "had to go outside." Spending 20 minutes outside each afternoon felt like drudgery, so they often skipped the playground to walk around the block instead.

Vince loved taking his class outdoors. His class could not get enough of the new climbing structure that had been recently donated to their school. With plenty of space to run, jump, hide, and climb, children were continually coming up with new games and ideas for play.

Every afternoon, Geri took the children in her class to run around on the grass field behind their playground. On warm afternoons, they would take walks through the trails behind the school. Being surrounded by nature gave children so much to look at and led to many exciting questions and conversations!

Whether your class's outdoor space most closely resembles Monique's, Vince's, or Geri's, outdoor time is another part of the day during which self-regulation can be practiced! Outdoor play offers many opportunities for embedding self-regulation practice into children's play (e.g., helping children learn to take turns on playground equipment or regulate their emotions during playground conflicts). Additionally, teachers can facilitate games and activities focused on self-regulation to promote active engagement in physical activity and to practice other skills (e.g., turn taking). A large body of research documents the importance of physical activity in young children (indoors and outdoors) for numerous outcomes, including physical health and reducing the risk of obesity as well as social and academic success. In this chapter, we share research on the importance of outdoor play and gross motor play. We discuss the benefits of gross motor play for children's outcomes and share ways that self-regulation can be embedded into gross motor play indoors and outdoors.

Time spent outdoors (or time spent engaging in gross motor play) serves many important purposes. For children, going outside is an opportunity to:

- Develop fine and gross motor skills
- Engage in unstructured play
- Explore the environment and gain an appreciation for the world around them
- Participate in exercise or physical activity
- Practice social skills (including self-regulation) through navigating social situations
- Problem-solve
- Release energy.

Sometimes teachers view outdoor time as a "break" during which they can socialize with other teachers, and generally devote less energy to monitoring children. Although finding times throughout your day to de-stress and replenish your own energy is important, this personal need must be balanced against the needs of the children. Just like time spent indoors, time spent outdoors is an important part of early childhood education. Teachers who remain engaged with children throughout the day—indoors and outdoors—help create teachable moments and learning opportunities out of even the most mundane times. Children need "down time" too so that they can explore the world around them and play independently as well as with other children. When we talk about being engaged with children, we are referring not only to being actively engaged in conversation and activities but also to being mindful of the experiences children have had throughout the day, so that you can support what they need in the moment (e.g., a structured activity or individual time to explore). Even during outdoor and gross motor play when children are happily running around, there are many instances that arise where children can benefit from support, modeling, or teaching related to self-regulation.

Ms. Luz watched as the other teachers on the playground stood together, keeping one eye on the playground while talking and laughing about their weekend plans. Rather than joining in, she positioned herself at the base of the slide. The slide had been an especially challenging area of the playground over the last week. Children routinely stepped over one another while trying to climb the stairs and pushed one another out of the way as they scrambled to be the first down the slide. Several children had been injured (nothing major—minor head bumps and bruises), so she wanted to be proactive, not only to keep children from getting hurt but also to help children develop the self-regulation skills they needed to navigate the playground equipment pro-socially. Ms. Luz asked each child who approached the slide to look and see if there was anyone else on the stairs. If no one else was climbing, the child was free to run up. If there was a friend climbing, she reminded the child to wait at the bottom of the steps and watch his or her friend go down the slide before climbing up the steps. After two weeks of monitoring the slide, Ms. Luz noticed that children were starting to wait at the bottom of the steps without being reminded and watching more carefully for others to finish before using the slide.

In this example, Ms. Luz positions herself in a way that she can embed self-regulation practice into playground time without interfering with children's ability to play creatively independently or together. Children playing on the slide are still taking the lead in guiding their own play and interactions, but Ms. Luz is interjecting herself to provide reminders ensuring that children are practicing and demonstrating self-regulation effectively. Like Ms. Luz, teachers can identify teachable moments in the midst of children's outdoor play or they can facilitate practice of self-regulation skills by facilitating gross motor activities outdoors or indoors. Both are valuable ways to promote self-regulation and physical activity.

●●●●●

Learning Checkpoint #1

Think about the outdoor space you have available at your center.

1. In what ways do you see children regularly exhibiting self-regulation on the playground?
2. Where on the playground or during what activities do you see children having the most difficulties with self-regulation?
3. What other opportunities (in addition to time outside) do children have to engage in gross motor play?
4. What do you do or what does your center do to provide children with gross motor activities when the weather does not permit you to go outside?

Physical Health and Obesity Prevention

Outdoor time (and gross motor play) is becoming increasingly important as concerns about childhood obesity increase. One study found that nearly 35% of adults and 17% of children (ages 2–19 years old) in the U.S. in 2010–11 were obese (Ogden, Carroll, Kit, & Flegal, 2014). Another study including 7,738 children who were followed from kindergarten through eighth grade found that at kindergarten entry, 12.4% of children were obese and another 14.9% were considered overweight. In the same study, children who were overweight in kindergarten were four times more likely than children at a normal weight to be obese when they reached middle school (Cunningham, Kramer, & Narayan, 2014). Alarmingly, childhood obesity is related to a wide range of health outcomes, including diabetes, heart disease, and certain cancers (Dixon, 2010).

Although there are many factors that contribute to childhood obesity, including poor dietary habits, food insufficiency or insecurity, and parental attitudes about food (Heath, 2013), we chose to focus specifically on physical activity in this chapter because of the connection between physical activity and the self-regulation activities presented in this book.

Providing children with opportunities to engage in physical activity through outdoor and gross motor play is critical for promoting physical health and preventing obesity (Hills, Andersen, & Byrne, 2011). Moreover, being physically active can help prevent a host of health problems in the short and long term (Trost, Blair, & Khan, 2014; Trost, Messner, Fitzgerald, & Roths, 2011). In addition to direct connections between physical activity and physical health, research has shown that physical activity and physical fitness have an impact on self-regulation and academic achievement (Centers for Disease Control and Prevention, 2010; Donnelly & Lambourne, 2011).

Importance of Physical Activity for Self-Regulation and Learning

An exciting line of research has looked at the links between physical activity, self-regulation, and early learning in children. This research is based on the idea that the body and brain need to work together in order to understand and interpret the world. This idea is called *embodied cognition* and describes the links between mind and body, explaining how perceptual and motor skills help facilitate cognitive development by representing and manipulating information (Becker, McClelland, Loprinzi, & Trost, 2014). In young children, embodied cognition is often seen in active play. A large body of research highlights the importance of play for young children's cognitive and social development (e.g., Hirsh-Pasek, Golinkoff, Berk, & Singer, 2008), and recent research has looked at how physically active play may benefit self-regulation in young children. In one study with preschoolers, more active play was related to better self-regulation, which in turn was related to higher reading and math skills (Becker et al., 2014). This suggests that helping children be more active, especially in play, can indirectly benefit school readiness through stronger self-regulation.

Importantly, studies are showing that exercise that is cognitively engaging is more likely to increase children's executive functioning than exercise that is not (Best, 2010). Similar findings are being found in later grades as well. Research on elementary school children have found that participating in short physical activity breaks throughout the school day can actually help children pay better attention to learning tasks at school (Janssen et al., 2014; Mahar, 2011).

Physical Activity in Preschool

Despite the importance of physical activity for preschoolers' social and academic outcomes, studies are finding that, in general, children attending preschool are not provided with adequate opportunity to engage in active play (McWilliams et al., 2009). In one study, preschoolers were observed throughout the day using a measure of activity level called the Observational System for Recording Physical Activity in Children–Preschool Version (Brown et al., 2006). Using this measure, 493 preschoolers were observed for a total of five hours each. Children were engaged in sedentary activities for 80% of the observations and in moderate-to-vigorous physical activity for less than 3% of the observations (Pate, McIver, Dowda, Brown, & Addy, 2008). Other studies have found the percentage of time children spend in sedentary activities to be as high as 89% of their time (Brown et al., 2009). Best practices for physical activity in preschool recommend that preschoolers participate in at least 60 minutes of active play during the preschool day, with some sources recommending 120 minutes (McWilliams et al., 2009; Tucker, 2008). A review of studies including over 10,000 children found that only 54% of children in these studies were meeting the recommended requirements for physical activity (Tucker, 2008). Even when examining just the time children spend outdoors, preschoolers are still primarily engaging in sedentary activities (56%) with 27% of their time spent in light activities and 17% spent in moderate-to-vigorous physical activity (Brown et al., 2009).

There are many factors that have the potential to impact children's engagement in physical activity in preschool settings. Studies have found that the physical environment at early childhood centers plays a role in children's activity level during play. For example, one study found that children's physical activity was higher in early childhood centers when more activities for active play were provided (e.g., more outdoor time; structured indoor activities including physical activity), children had access to play equipment (both portable play equipment and fixed play equipment), and staff had training in physical education and activities (Bower et al., 2008). These findings suggest that there is room for educators to increase their involvement in children's active play to help facilitate moderate-to-vigorous physical activity

(Brown et al., 2009). Increasing children's physical activity can be a challenge, however! Surveys of early childhood educators have found that educators experience many barriers to providing children with physical activity opportunities. Barriers include limited access to outdoor space, parent concerns about children getting injured, pressure from administration to focus primarily on academics, and personal preference to avoid the outdoors (Copeland, Kendeigh, Saelens, Kalkwarf, & Sherman, 2012; Copeland, Sherman, Kendeigh, Kalkwarf, & Saelens, 2012). For example, some educators reported that they did not like extreme hot or cold weather, getting dirty, or the chaos of the playground. Educators also shared in their surveys that they believed physical activity was important for children and that they saw many benefits, including gross motor development, self-confidence and self-regulation, better attention, and better naps after children participated in exercise (Copeland, Kendeigh, et al., 2012).

●●●●●

Learning Checkpoint #2

1. How much time do you think children in your class or at your center spend engaging in gross motor or outdoor play? What barriers do you and your class face to getting enough time outdoors?
2. What is one thing you can do to increase the time children spend engaging in moderate-to-vigorous physical activity?

Overview of Interventions that have Targeted Physical Activity

Research has shown that interventions and programs can have positive effects on increasing children's physical activity throughout childhood and adolescence (Trost et al., 2014). Much of the work to date has focused on older children and helping keep them active as a way to reduce obesity in children and youth, although some research with young children is emerging (Trost et al., 2011). In addition to positive effects on healthy eating and increased physical activity, some of these studies also find that elementary and middle school students who participate in more vigorous activity achieve higher grades (Donnelly et al., 2009; Donnelly & Lambourne, 2011) and math achievement (Davis et al., 2011). These effects have also been found for younger children where higher levels of aerobic fitness have been linked to higher math and reading achievement (Castelli, Hillman, Buck, & Erwin, 2007; Eveland-Sayers, Farley, Fuller, Morgan, & Caputo, 2009). Although little research has incorporated self-regulation into these physical activity interventions, the research that is available suggests that interventions and programs that include an explicit focus on self-regulation and games can be effective in promoting physical activity, self-regulation, and school success in children. Following this chapter is an "Activity Break" where we provide specific activities designed to promote self-regulation through active play in fine and gross motor activities. Many of the games can be played indoors or outdoors and can be modified for small or large groups.

Reflect

Knowing that most children do not engage in the recommended amount of physical activity, what is one thing you can do to help the children in your class increase the time they spend in outdoor or gross motor play?

Set a Goal

Choose at least two activities presented in "Activity Break #4: Self-Regulation Games in Outdoor and Gross Motor Play" to try in your classroom. After trying the activities, reflect on children's response to them. What went well? What challenges did you experience? How would you modify the activities next time?

• • • • •

Additional Resources

See Chapter 9 for additional resources related to the contents of this chapter, including Internet resources focusing on outdoor and gross motor play and recommended children's books focusing on outdoor and gross motor play.

• • • • •

References

Becker, D. R., McClelland, M. M., Loprinzi, P., & Trost, S. G. (2014). Physical activity, self-regulation, and early academic achievement in preschool children. *Early Education and Development, 25*(1), 56–70. doi:10.1080/10409289.2013.780505

Best, J. R. (2010). Effects of physical activity on children's executive function: Contributions of experimental research on aerobic exercise. *Developmental Review, 30*(4), 331–351.

Bower, J. K., Hales, D. P., Tate, D. F., Rubin, D. A., Benjamin, S. E., & Ward, D. S. (2008). The childcare environment and children's physical activity. *American Journal of Preventive Medicine, 34*(1), 23–29.

Brown, W. H., Pfeiffer, K. A., McIver, K. L., Dowda, M., Addy, C. L., & Pate, R. R. (2009). Social and environmental factors associated with preschoolers' nonsedentary physical activity. *Child Development, 80*(1), 45–58.

Brown, W. H., Pfeiffer, K. A., McIver, K. L., Dowda, M., Almeida, J. M., & Pate, R. R. (2006). Assessing preschool children's physical activity: The Observational System for Recording Physical Activity in Children–preschool version. *Research Quarterly for Exercise and Sport, 77*(2), 167–176.

Castelli, D. M., Hillman, C. H., Buck, S. M., & Erwin, H. E. (2007). Physical fitness and academic achievement in third- and fifth-grade students. *Journal of Sport & Exercise Psychology, 29*(2), 239–252.

Centers for Disease Control and Prevention. (2010). *The association between school-based physical activity, including physical education, and academic performance*. Atlanta, GA: U.S. Department of Health and Human Services.

Copeland, K. A., Kendeigh, C. A., Saelens, B. E., Kalkwarf, H. J., & Sherman, S. N. (2012). Physical activity in child-care centers: Do teachers hold the key to the playground? *Health Education Research, 27*(1), 81–100. doi:10.1093/her/cyr038

Copeland, K. A., Sherman, S. N., Kendeigh, C. A., Kalkwarf, H. J., & Saelens, B. E. (2012). Societal values and policies may curtail preschool children's physical activity in child care centers. *Pediatrics, 129*(2), 265–274. doi:10.1542/peds.2011-2102

Cunningham, S. A., Kramer, M. R., & Narayan, K. V. (2014). Incidence of childhood obesity in the United States. *New England Journal of Medicine, 370*(5), 403–411.

Davis, C. L., Tomporowski, P. D., McDowell, J. E., Austin, B. P., Miller, P. H., Yanasak, N. E., . . . Naglieri, J. A. (2011). Exercise improves executive function and achievement and alters brain activation in overweight children: A randomized, controlled trial. *Health Psychology, 30*(1), 91–98. doi:10.1037=a0021766

Dixon, J. B. (2010). The effect of obesity on health outcomes. *Molecular and Cellular Endocrinology, 316*(2), 104–108.

Donnelly, J. E., Greene, J. L., Gibson, C. A., Smith, B. K., Washburn, R. A., Sullivan, D. K., . . . Williams, S. L. (2009). Physical Activity Across the Curriculum (PAAC): A randomized controlled trial to promote physical activity and diminish overweight and obesity in elementary school children. *Preventive Medicine, 49*, 336–341. doi:10.1016=j.ypmed.2009.07.022

Donnelly, J. E., & Lambourne, K. (2011). Classroom-based physical activity, cognition, and academic achievement. *Preventive Medicine: An International Journal Devoted to Practice and Theory, 52*(Suppl), S36–S42. doi:10.1016/j.ypmed.2011.01.021

Eveland-Sayers, B. M., Farley, R. S., Fuller, D. K., Morgan, D. W., & Caputo, J. L. (2009). Physical fitness and academic achievement in elementary school children. *Journal of Physical Activity & Health, 6*(1), 99–104.

Heath, P. (2013). *Parent-child relations: Context, research, and application* (3rd ed.). Boston, MA: Pearson.

Hills, A. P., Andersen, L. B., & Byrne, N. M. (2011). Physical activity and obesity in children. *British Journal of Sports Medicine, 45*(11), 866–870.

Hirsh-Pasek, K., Golinkoff, R. M., Berk, L. E., & Singer, D. G. (Eds.). (2009). *A mandate for playful learning in preschool: Presenting the evidence*. New York, NY: Oxford University Press.

Janssen, M., Chinapaw, M., Rauh, S., Toussaint, H., van Mechelen, W., & Verhagen, E. (2014). A short physical activity break from cognitive tasks increases selective attention in primary school children aged 10–11. *Mental Health and Physical Activity, 7*(3), 129–134.

Mahar, M. T. (2011). Impact of short bouts of physical activity on attention-to-task in elementary school children. *Preventive Medicine, 52*, S60–S64.

McWilliams, C., Ball, S. C., Benjamin, S. E., Hales, D., Vaughn, A., & Ward, D. S. (2009). Best-practice guidelines for physical activity at child care. *Pediatrics, 124*(6), 1650–1659.

Ogden, C. L., Carroll, M. D., Kit, B. K., & Flegal, K. M. (2014). Prevalence of childhood and adult obesity in the United States, 2011–2012. *Journal of the American Medical Association, 311*(8), 806–814.

Pate, R. R., McIver, K., Dowda, M., Brown, W. H., & Addy, C. (2008). Directly observed physical activity levels in preschool children. *Journal of School Health, 78*(8), 438–444.

Trost, S. G., Blair, S. N., & Khan, K. M. (2014). Physical inactivity remains the greatest public health problem of the 21st century: Evidence, improved methods and solutions using the "7 investments that work" as a framework. *British Journal of Sports Medicine, 48*(3), 169–170. doi:10.1136/bjsports-2013–093372

Trost, S. G., Messner, L., Fitzgerald, K., & Roths, B. (2011). A nutrition and physical activity intervention for family child care homes. *American Journal of Preventive Medicine, 41*(4), 392–398. doi:10.1016/j.amepre.2011.06.030

Tucker, P. (2008). The physical activity levels of preschool-aged children: A systematic review. *Early Childhood Research Quarterly, 23*(4), 547–558.

ACTIVITY BREAK #4: SELF-REGULATION GAMES IN OUTDOOR AND GROSS MOTOR PLAY

Many traditional children's playground games (e.g., Red Light, Green Light; Mother May I?; Red Rover, Red Rover) focus on self-regulation, requiring children to stop and go and use inhibitory control in response to visual or oral cues. These traditional games are often competitive in nature, and although some children enjoy competitive games, others do not. The games presented here focus on collaborative and cooperative outcomes, allowing all children to participate in a way that enables them to be engaged regardless of their developmental level and to feel successful. Most of these games can be played outdoors or indoors with slight modifications depending on the space available. Many are also good for circle time!

Cooperative Freeze

(Circle time, gross motor play, or outdoor play)

Materials:

- CD player (optional; see Variation #1)
- CD with songs of varying tempos (slow and fast songs)
- Carpet squares (alternative: six large pieces of butcher paper taped to the classroom floor).

Procedure: This game is similar to the Freeze Dance (also presented in this activity break). Children are asked to dance when the music is playing and perform a specific action when the music stops. Explain to children that when the music stops, they should freeze and then find a carpet square to stand on. Together with children, count the number of carpet squares and the number of children in the classroom. Help children notice that there are not enough carpet squares for each child to have their own, so they will have to share. After playing the game a few rounds, remove one of the carpet squares. Talk with children about the importance of helping everyone find a space. Continue removing carpet squares until there are only two left. Suggest that children put only one foot on a carpet square to make room for their friends. Celebrate finding a way to fit everyone on just two carpet squares. This game can be modified to align with classroom themes. For example, if the classroom theme is outer space, use butcher paper cut in the shapes of planets. Tell children that they are pretending to be rockets and flying in space when the music plays. When the music stops, their rockets need to find a planet to land on.

Skill development: In this game, children are required to attend to the instructions of the game and use their working memory through keeping these instructions in mind as the game progresses. Children practice inhibitory control, not only through starting and stopping to musical cues but also by finding a place on the mat while intentionally making space for their peers. Children also practice spatial awareness of themselves and others as well as early math skills through counting and numeracy.

Cooperative Freeze Variation #1

To modify this game for outdoor play, lay six towels or pieces of fabric on the ground in your outdoor space. Use a smartphone to provide music or choose one of your class's favorite songs to sing out loud (e.g., "Pop Goes the Weasel"). Sing or play a song while children run in a large circle around the towels. When the song ends, children freeze and find a towel to stand on.

Drum Beats

(Circle time, gross motor play, or outdoor play)

Materials:

■ Classroom drum (alternate: inverted trash can or laundry hamper).

Procedure: Have children walk around the room or a designated outdoor space as you beat on the drum and freeze when the drumbeats stop. You can ask children to walk quickly (or run) to fast drumbeats and slowly (or tiptoe) to slow drumbeats and even to do the opposite (walk quickly to slow drumbeats and slowly to fast drumbeats).

Skill development: In this activity, children are required to attend to a complex set of directions. This game is especially taxing on children's working memory, requiring them to remember the actions represented by each drum cue. Children also practice inhibitory control by stopping and starting based on cues from the drum as well as fine and gross motor skills and spatial awareness of themselves and their peers.

Drum Beats Variation #1

If your class size is too large (or your space is too small) to allow children to walk around the room, substitute actions that can be done while staying in one place, such as kicking legs in the air, stomping feet, or clapping hands. See Figure 6.1 for an image of a child playing Drum Beats.

Figure 6.1 A Child Playing the Drum Beats Game.
Photo by Mackenzie Rice.

Freeze Dancing

(Circle time, gross motor play, or music and movement)

Materials:

- CD player
- CD with songs of different tempos (slow and fast; suggested songs are provided in Chapter 9).

Procedure: In this game, children dance when the music plays and freeze when the music stops. The teacher should pause the music periodically or switch between songs of different tempos. To increase the complexity of the game, play music that is a range of different speeds (slow and fast) and ask children to move slowly to slow songs and quickly to fast songs. To make the game even more complicated, ask children to dance slowly to fast songs and quickly to slow songs.

Skill development: This activity requires children to pay attention to the rules of the game as well as to the aural cues that are provided by the music. Children have to practice working memory to remember the rules of the game, particularly if the rules change during the activity, and children practice inhibitory control through starting and stopping to musical cues as well as in performing behaviors that are opposite to their impulses (dancing slowly to a fast song).

Freeze Dancing Variation #1

Identify songs that sound like animals (e.g., "Flight of the Bumblebee" by Rimsky-Korsakov or "Carnival of the Animals" by Saint-Saëns). Play Freeze Dancing using these songs, but instead of dancing, have children move like the animals depicted by the songs. Children will have to exercise their working memory to remember what animal was paired with what song. See Figure 6.2 for an image of two children playing Freeze Dancing.

Figure 6.2 Two Children Playing Freeze Dancing.
Photo by Mackenzie Rice.

Red Light, Purple Light

(Circle time, gross motor play, or outdoor play)

Materials:

- Different colors of construction paper cut into various shapes (e.g., red, blue, and purple circles, triangles, and squares).

Procedure: Similar to the traditional game, Red Light, Green Light, a teacher uses colors to indicate stop and go. Teachers should choose actions that are appropriate for the space (e.g., running if playing outdoors, marching or jumping in place if playing indoors). To start, choose an action (running in place) and choose two colors (e.g., a red circle and a purple circle). Tell children that the purple circle means "go" and the red circle means "stop." Hold the circles behind your back. Hold up one circle at a time, encouraging children to run in place when you hold up the purple circle and stop or freeze when you hold up the red circle. To make this game more challenging, switch colors—now red is "go" and purple is "stop."

Skill development: This game helps children practice paying attention to complex sets of instructions. Children also practice working memory through remembering which color/shape represents which action and inhibitory control through starting and stopping to the appropriate cues. Additional skills targeted by this game include fine and gross motor skills as well as shapes and colors.

Red Light, Purple Light Variation #1

In addition to using different colors to indicate stop and go, try using different shapes. For example, use an orange square, a blue square, an orange triangle, and a blue triangle. Tell children that any square is "stop" and any triangle is "go!" Once children catch on, try the opposite—any square is "go" and any triangle is "stop!"

Red Light, Purple Light Variation #2

Rather than just using stop and go, choose multiple actions. For example, a red circle can mean "clap your hands," and a yellow triangle can mean "shake your head." You can also use the same action, but at different speeds—green circle means "stomp your feet quickly," and a yellow circle means "stomp your feet slowly."

7

• • • • •

Engaging Families in Self-Regulation Development

Ms. Winter found it interesting to watch parents at the end of the school day. Some parents walked through the door and never made eye contact with a teacher, taking their child's backpack and hand and walking out of the door, all while talking on the phone. Other parents entered the classroom and took a lot of time to greet teachers and their child as they packed up for the day. The classroom cubby area was very small. Some parents pushed their way in to collect their child's coat and backpack without giving much attention to those around them, while others stood to the side and waited for a space to become available before taking a turn. Although Ms. Winter understood and valued that each family was different, she saw distinct differences in the self-regulation skills parents were modeling for their children even in these brief interactions.

Just like educators, parents and family members have many opportunities throughout the day to model self-regulation skills for children. When families understand the importance of self-regulation and their role in supporting children's self-regulation growth and development, they can turn these moments into valuable learning opportunities. In addition to modeling, parents can adopt parenting approaches and strategies that lay a foundation for strong self-regulation and introduce activities and games to help children strengthen these skills at home. In Chapter 2, we discussed how self-regulation develops, with an emphasis on the role of parents and family members as well as educators. In this chapter, we will extend that conversation and share ways that you can engage families in supporting children's self-regulation growth and development. Appreciating the essential role of families in child development helps educators understand the context in which each child is growing up, build and maintain trusting relationships with the parents and caregivers of the children in their classrooms, and ultimately share information about the child across school and home contexts in a way that is respectful and mutually supportive, promoting children's social and academic success (LaRocque, Kleiman, & Darling, 2011).

● ● ● ● ●

The Role of Families in Self-Regulation Development

In Chapter 2, we talked about how self-regulation develops—shifting from an external to an internal process in the context of children's relationships with the adults in their lives. Not surprisingly, many of the strategies we presented for educators are the same for parents and family members. Parents who develop secure attachment relationships with their children, demonstrate an authoritative parenting style, model strong self-regulation skills, and actively teach these skills to children optimize children's self-regulation development. Numerous theoretical perspectives highlight the important role that families play in children's self-regulation development. One in particular, the bioecological model of human development, is often cited to support the role of families in children's growth and development.

According to the bioecological model of human development, development occurs within a system (Bronfenbrenner & Morris, 2006). A child is at the center of the system at a level called the "microsystem." Around the child is a level called the "mesosystem," which represents the environment and relationships a child has at home and at school. Beyond the mesosystem is the exosystem (e.g., economic and political system), macrosystem (e.g., overarching societal beliefs), and chronosystem (e.g., time). Although research supports the notion that each level of the system influences each of the other levels, the child's immediate family and caregivers are closest to the center of the system and thus have the most direct and immediate impact on a child, particularly in early childhood.

Applying this theory to self-regulation, we can think of many ways that parents and family members can shape children's development. Just like early childhood educators, parents lay a foundation for self-regulation development through building secure attachment relationships, using an authoritative parenting style that encourages autonomy, and modeling and teaching self-regulation skills (McClelland, Ponitz, Messersmith, & Tominey, 2010). For example, there are many ways that parents and family members can model self-regulation throughout the day, including:

■ Putting electronic devices (e.g., computers, tablets, smartphones) aside to have conversations or play games with children during family time;
■ Balancing work and family life;
■ Modeling waiting for a turn (e.g., waiting to wash their hands until after children finish);

- Making a dessert and waiting until after dinner to eat it (delayed gratification);
- Using private speech out loud and talking about what they are doing and why;
- Explaining boundaries and consequences to children as well as why they are being disciplined (authoritative parenting style);
- Managing sibling conflict appropriately;
- Creating bedtime rituals and routines together with children.

Parents can also play games with children at home that promote self-regulation, including many of the games presented in the activity breaks in this book.

Recognizing the role of families in the lives of young children is critical for early childhood educators. Realizing that all families have different backgrounds and experiences as well as different levels of resources available to them (e.g., time, knowledge, materials, education) can help educators avoid blaming families for a child's challenging behaviors or for challenges in the child's life and instead effectively support the family's role and engagement in their child's learning at school.

● ● ● ● ●

The Importance of Engaging Families in Early Childhood Education

Engaging families in children's school experiences in early childhood has many benefits for children's learning and development and lays the foundation for a family's continued involvement in their child's schooling. Preschool is one of the first classroom environments that most children experience (Phillips, McCartney, & Sussman, 2006), so for many families, preschool is their first opportunity to be engaged in their child's learning outside of the home. This places a tremendous responsibility on early childhood educators. Providing families with an experience where they feel welcome and supported can shape the way families approach school engagement as children enter kindergarten and continue into elementary school and beyond. Fortunately, the early childhood years are a time when children welcome their parents' involvement and presence at school (Hornby & Lafaele, 2011). Promoting family engagement in children's early learning can support children's self-regulation development as well as many other social and academic outcomes.

• • • • •

The Benefits of Family Engagement in Early Childhood Education

When he picked Muhammed up each afternoon, Muhammed's dad took time to walk around the classroom and look at the activities Muhammed had participated in throughout the day. Muhammed proudly showed his dad a new piece of art he had made that was hanging on the wall.

To share a special family tradition and celebrate Chinese New Year, Ping's mom came to her daughter's class to read a book and lead the children in a dumpling-making activity.

Although she rarely had the opportunity to visit her daughter's classroom, Molly's mom always asked her about her day and thought of games they could play at home that aligned with topics Molly was learning about at school.

Family involvement can take many forms. The foregoing examples are just a few of the ways parents might be involved in their children's early education. Involvement can happen at school (e.g., volunteering at or visiting school, attending school functions, participating in classroom activities), at home (e.g., engaging a child in home learning activities), through serving on a school committee (e.g., parent group, school board), and in other ways (LaRocque et al., 2011).

Supporting family engagement in your classroom is important for many reasons. Research shows that family engagement relates to numerous social and academic outcomes for children, including increased academic achievement and graduation rates (Jeynes, 2012; LaRocque et al., 2011; Wilder, 2014). For example, one study found that the number of school-based activities parents participated in while their child was in preschool and kindergarten was associated with higher reading achievement in eighth grade as well as lower rates of grade retention (Miedel & Reynolds, 1999). Another study found that parent involvement in kindergarten predicted gains in children's reading and math skills across the school year (Galindo & Sheldon, 2012). A third study found that family involvement was related to children's literacy skills in a sample of Latino families (Durand, 2011). Together, these studies highlight the importance of family involvement in promoting children's short- and long-term school success. Not only does parent engagement benefit children, but also it has benefits for teachers. For example, educators who build supportive relationships with parents and caregivers improve the line of communication between school and home. Regular communication between parents and educators can help educators learn about children across the home and school context, enabling them to better support children at school.

This communication can also support families' abilities to extend learning that happens at school to home. As we have discussed, there are many benefits to family engagement, but there are also many barriers that might impact a family's ability to be involved.

● ● ● ● ●

Barriers to Family Engagement

Despite the evidence that family engagement is important, there are many reasons why being actively involved in their child's school can be a challenge for families. Barriers to school involvement can include family factors (e.g., parental beliefs about involvement, challenging life contexts, not feeling invited), child factors (e.g., behavioral challenges), parent-teacher relationship factors (e.g., different languages spoken or different perceived goals), and societal factors (Hornby & Lafaele, 2011). In one study conducted with mothers who had children enrolled in Head Start, having a schedule that conflicted with activities, having a young child at home (infant or toddler), and feeling a lack of energy or low interest also served as barriers to school involvement (Lamb-Parker et al., 2001). Numerous studies show that economic stress in a family also relates to low parent involvement (Waanders, Mendez, & Downer, 2007).

● ● ● ● ●

Learning Checkpoint #1

1. Make a list of all the stressors parents and caregivers of the children in your classroom might experience during a typical day. How do you think experiencing one or more of these stressors might impact their ability to be actively engaged in their child's school? How do you think acknowledging the many stressors families experience might help you support their engagement in school?

● ● ● ● ●

Promoting Classroom Engagement While Appreciating Family Diversity

Having an awareness of the stressors families face in their daily lives and of the barriers families may face to active involvement is an important step toward effectively engaging families from a wide range of backgrounds. No two families are alike. Even families from the same socioeconomic, linguistic, or cultural background are different from one another! Moreover, what works well for one family may not work for another—no matter how similar or different they are, which can create challenges for early childhood educators. Reaching out to families throughout the day and over the school year in many different ways increases the chances of finding a way of effectively involving each family (or as many families as possible)—even if engagement looks different for each family. Educators who appreciate many different forms of family involvement and provide families with numerous and varied opportunities to be engaged can facilitate a family's ability to support their child's self-regulation growth and development. In the next section, we provide specific tips for effectively engaging families and promoting family involvement in children's self-regulation development.

Tips for Effectively Engaging Families to Support Children's Self-Regulation Development

1. *Foster a classroom community for children as well as for parents.* Parents who feel welcome at school and who have better communication with other classroom parents are more engaged in their child's school (Durand, 2011). Creating a classroom community for children and for parents will help.

   a. Take time to connect with parents on a regular basis. It may not be possible to connect with every classroom parent on a daily basis, but intentionally connecting with each parent on a rotating basis or dividing parent conversations among classroom teachers can help build relationships between educators and parents.

   b. Help parents connect with one another. Take time to introduce parents to one another at pickup and drop-off or during school functions. Provide a classroom directory (with parent permission) to help parents connect with one another and build connections and support outside of school.

   c. Provide materials for parents in their home language. Even something as simple as handwriting a sign on the door that says "Welcome" in each of the different languages represented in your classroom can set the tone of the classroom environment.

2. *Create a classroom that serves as a learning environment for children and parents/caregivers.* There are many ways that you can engage parents in children's self-regulation development by embedding learning activities into parent-child routines during pickup and drop-off (this may not be possible if the majority of children are bussed to your school).

   a. Display classroom schedules with accompanying pictures in a place where children and parents will see them during their drop-off and pickup routines. If schedules or routines (e.g., hand-washing and hanging up coats) are accompanied by images, children can play a role in explaining these routines to their parents, modeling their own self-regulation abilities.

3. *Provide parents with resources to support their own knowledge of self-regulation development.*

   a. Create bulletin boards or classroom newsletters that provide parents with resources related to children's self-regulation development as well as specific strategies they can use at home to promote self-regulation.

   b. Build a self-regulation resource library for parents and caregivers. Maintain a list of web-based resources (e.g., articles, video clips) as well as physical books that parents can check out. Provide books in other languages (e.g., Spanish) if they are available.

4. *Provide information in formats that are relevant to families.* Consider the barriers that families may face in being able to benefit from the resources you provide.

   a. What languages do families in your classroom speak? Can you find resources available for families in these languages or is translation help available?

   b. What is the literacy level of parents in your classroom? Are the materials provided at a reading level comfortable for and supportive of all families? Providing materials in a range of formats (e.g., reading materials, video clips, Internet links) will help maximize the number of parents who will be reached by these resources.

5. *Be creative in the ways that you reach out to parents.* In addition to traditional methods of reaching out to parents (e.g., classroom newsletter, parent-teacher conferences, informal conversations at pickup and drop-off), consider non-traditional ways of sharing information.

   a. Create interactive bulletin boards where parents not only learn new information but also are invited to contribute to the discussion through posting their own ideas or resources. Ask parents to share games that they play with children at home. Many of these games may help promote self-regulation! Now that you have a foundation in the components of self-regulation, you can help parents identify the skills these games are promoting.

6. *Engage children in teaching their parents and caregivers.* Teaching children songs or games that they can teach their parents may be an effective way to engage parents in self-regulation activities with their children at home. For example, Mirror, Mirror (Activity Break #1) and ABCs—loud and soft (Activity Break #3) are simple games children

could learn at school and teach their parents at home. Sending home a handout with instructions for the games may help parents clarify rules or instructions that children have difficulties explaining.

7. *Invite parents and caregivers to attend "learn with me" activities.* Inviting parents and caregivers into the classroom is a great way to teach them self-regulation games and activities that they can use at home. Nearly all of the games and activities presented in this book can be slightly modified for families to play at home with one or more children. Consider holding a family game night or an activity where parents are invited into the classroom to engage in playing games with children. Provide handouts with descriptions of the games so that parents can continue playing with children and helping them practice self-regulation at home.

Reflect

How would you like families to feel in your classroom? What do you do (or what can you do) to promote these feelings for families of the children in your class or in your future classroom?

Set a Goal

Identify at least two new strategies presented in this chapter that you would like to try in your classroom to promote family involvement. After trying these strategies, reflect on what went well. Were you able to engage families in new ways or families who had not been previously involved? What challenges did you experience with involvement?

● ● ● ● ●

Additional Resources

See Chapter 9 for additional resources related to the contents of this chapter, including Internet resources focusing on engaging families and promoting self-regulation at home; recommended self-regulation books to build your parent library; and recommended children's books to support secure child and family relationships.

● ● ● ● ●

References

Bronfenbrenner, U., & Morris, P.A. (2006). The bioecological model of human development. In *Handbook of child psychology: Vol. 1. Theoretical models of human development* (6th ed., pp. 793–828). Hoboken, NJ: Wiley.

Durand, T.M. (2011). Latino parental involvement in kindergarten findings from the Early Childhood Longitudinal Study. *Hispanic Journal of Behavioral Sciences, 33*(4), 469–489.

Galindo, C., & Sheldon, S.B. (2012). School and home connections and children's kindergarten achievement gains: The mediating role of family involvement. *Early Childhood Research Quarterly, 27*(1), 90–103.

Hornby, G., & Lafaele, R. (2011). Barriers to parental involvement in education: An explanatory model. *Educational Review, 63*(1), 37–52.

Jeynes, W. (2012). A meta-analysis of the efficacy of different types of parental involvement programs for urban students. *Urban Education, 47*(4), 706–742.

Lamb-Parker, F., Piotrkowski, C.S., Baker, A.J.L., Kessler-Sklar, S., Clark, B., & Peay, L. (2001). Understanding barriers to parent involvement in Head Start: A research-community partnership. *Early Childhood Research Quarterly, 16*(1), 35–51. doi:10.1016/S0885–2006(01)00084–9

LaRocque, M., Kleiman, I., & Darling, S.M. (2011). Parental involvement: The missing link in school achievement. *Preventing School Failure, 55*(3), 115–122.

McClelland, M.M., Ponitz, C.C., Messersmith, E.E., & Tominey, S. (2010). Self-regulation: The integration of cognition and emotion. In R. Lerner (Series Ed.) & W. Overton (Vol. Ed.), *Handbook of lifespan human development: Vol. 1. Cognition, biology and methods* (pp. 509–553). Hoboken, NJ: John Wiley.

Miedel, W.T., & Reynolds, A.J. (1999). Parent involvement in early intervention for disadvantaged children: Does it matter? *Journal of School Psychology, 37*(4), 379–402. doi:10.1016/S0022–4405(99)00023–0

Phillips, D., McCartney, K., & Sussman, A. (2006). Child care and early development. In K. McCartney & D. Phillips (Eds.), *Blackwell handbook of early childhood development* (pp. 471–489). Malden, MA: Blackwell.

Waanders, C., Mendez, J.L., & Downer, J.T. (2007). Parent characteristics, economic stress and neighborhood context as predictors of parent involvement in preschool children's education. *Journal of School Psychology, 45*(6), 619–636. doi:10.1016/j.jsp.2007.07.003

Wilder, S. (2014). Effects of parental involvement on academic achievement: A meta-synthesis. *Educational Review, 66*(3), 377–397.

8
• • • • •

Self-Regulation Assessment and Intervention

Jordan is four and a half. Even though he is easily distracted and has trouble sitting still during circle time, he loves to paint. He could paint independently at the easel for an hour!

Lily just turned three. She is slow to warm up and is often called "shy." Because she is so quiet, she never draws negative attention from her teachers, who assume she is always following directions and paying attention.

Three-and-a-half-year-old Malik has a permanent grin on his face. When asked to do something, he always responds by saying, "Yes!" Even though he is always eager to do what he is asked, he seems to be behind his peers academically, struggling with basic concepts, such as colors and shapes.

Adrianna just turned five and is the oldest child in her preschool class. She knows the classroom routine well and is often praised for being a good helper. Her teachers are frustrated, however, that when she gets upset, Adrianna reacts aggressively by hitting and pushing her classmates.

These examples highlight some of the ways that self-regulation emerges (or fails to emerge) in early childhood. Although we have a strong understanding of what a typical trajectory of self-regulation development looks like, it is important to remember that each child is different. Every child follows a unique developmental path, demonstrates unique strengths, and experiences different challenges. With so much variability within and between children, how do we know whether children have the self-regulation skills they need for success?

Is Jordan's ability to focus on painting for an extended period of time indicative of his future study habits, or is his inability to sit still at circle time a red flag? Are children like Lily and Malik destined to be strong students because they appear to follow directions and thus draw only positive attention, or are they at risk of falling through the cracks because no one notices when they are not paying attention and thus not actively engaged in learning? How will Adrianna's difficulties with self-regulation in social relationships impact her ability to get along with others and her ability to learn?

In this chapter, we discuss ways in which the field of early childhood is developing an understanding of the answers to these questions and others. Specifically, we share an overview of how children's self-regulation skills are currently being measured in early childhood, providing tips for assessing children's self-regulation in your own classroom. We conclude by sharing tips for assessing self-regulation in your classroom and at your center.

● ● ● ● ●

Assessing Self-Regulation in Early Childhood

There are many reasons why early childhood educators might want to measure children's self-regulation abilities. Measuring children's self-regulation can help educators:

1. Plan activities and learning experiences that support the growth and development of self-regulation skills;
2. Identify delays or deficits that require extra support or the need for special services;
3. Measure how effective a program or curriculum is at promoting self-regulation skills to make sure expected growth is actually happening (Gullo, 2005).

Each of these reasons for conducting assessments also can be applied to other learning areas (e.g., emergent literacy, early math skills). Self-regulation, however, is a skill that often stands out because it relates directly to children's behavior in the classroom.

Sam is in his third week of school and has already had two instances of problematic behaviors, including causing the toilet to overflow and throwing his shoe at a teacher. Sam's classroom has two teachers and 19 children, and his behavior is causing serious disruptions throughout the day. His teachers do not want to give up on Sam, but they are struggling with how to help him and also meet the needs of the other children in the class.

This example may be all too familiar to early childhood educators. Sam's teachers would likely say that Sam is struggling with self-regulation, but they might not know what to do about it or they may feel that it is challenging or impossible to give Sam the support he needs with so many other children in the class. Observing children informally in their interactions with others and during the school day can provide teachers with valuable information about their self-regulation abilities. There are other ways to measure self-regulation as well. The most common approaches include observations, survey reports from others (e.g., teachers or parents/caregivers), and direct assessments with children. Each of these methods has its strengths and limitations. In the following section, we share a brief overview of the types of assessments that are used to measure self-regulation and provide specific examples of each. Table 8.1 provides a list of many different measures that are used to assess self-regulation in early childhood.

Table 8.1 Examples of Early Childhood Self-Regulation Assessments

Measure name	Measure overview
Observational Measures	
Individualized Classroom Assessment Scoring System (InCLASS; Downer et al., 2010)	An observation system that measures the quality of a child's interactions with tasks, teachers, and peers in different classroom settings, and includes a dimension of children's behavioral control and self-regulation
Observed Classroom Engagement Scale (OCES; Rimm-Kaufmann et al., 2005)	An observational tool that measures children's engagement in learning during classroom activities including self-regulation
Parent/Educator Surveys	
Ages and Stages Questionnaire (ASQ; Squires & Bricker, 2009)	A series of parent-report, age-graded developmental screening instruments that assess aspects of self-regulation and social development
Child Behavior Checklist (CBC; Achenback & Rescorla, 2000)	A child behavior rating scale for assessing behavior problems, including internalizing and externalizing problems
Child Behavior Rating Scale (CBRS; Bronson et al., 1995)	A teacher rating scale that assesses children's self-regulation and social competence
Cooper-Farran Behavior Rating Scales (Cooper & Farran, 1988)	A teacher rating scale that assesses children's work-related and interpersonal skills in classroom settings
Devereux Early Childhood Assessment for Preschoolers (DECA; LeBuffe & Naglieri, 2012)	A teacher and parent-rated assessment that measures children's initiative, self-regulation, and attachment/relationships
Direct Assessments	
Bear and Dragon (Carlson, 2005)	Measures inhibitory control using puppets; children are given commands by a bear and dragon puppet, and respond only to the bear's commands.
Dimensional Change Card Sorting Task (DCCS; Zelazo, 2006)	A cognitive flexibility task that asks children to sort by different categories
Attention Network Task (Rueda, Rothbart, McCandliss, Saccomanno, & Posner, 2005)	A flanker task assessing attention where children feed the fish by pressing a button corresponding to the direction in which the middle fish is swimming

(Continued)

Table 8.1 (Continued)

Measure name	Measure overview
Head-Toes-Knees-Shoulders Task (HTKS; McClelland et al., 2014)	An opposite Simon-Says game where children do the opposite of a given command; the task measures attention, inhibitory control, and working memory
Preschool Self-Regulation Assessment (PSRA; Smith-Donald, Raver, Hayes, & Richardson, 2007)	A self-regulation battery that measures emotional and cognitive aspects of regulation
Snack Delay (Kochanska, Coy, & Murray, 2001)	A delay of gratification measure that assesses emotion regulation and asks children to wait for a reward (snack)
Turtle and Rabbit (Kochanska et al., 2001)	A measure of inhibitory control where children have to use their motor skills to slow down or speed up by moving a turtle or rabbit along a curved path

Observational Assessments

Observational assessment refers to the act of observing a child or a group of children in a controlled setting (laboratory) or a natural-istic setting (classroom or home). Observations can be informal or formal. Informal observations are less structured and are the most familiar way to assess children's self-regulation skills for many early childhood educators. Most educators conduct informal observa-tions throughout the day as they observe children in the classroom individually and during interactions with peers and adults. When conducting informal assessments, teachers rely on their own knowl-edge of child development and particularly their knowledge of typical development to determine when a child's behavior requires support beyond what can typically be provided in early childhood classrooms. Informal observations have many benefits. First, teach-ers spend many hours with children and get to know them very well. Second, teachers have exposure to many children and thus can compare the skills of one child against the skills of others in the classroom to determine when a behavior is problematic or a child has a skill deficit. Informal observations are typically conducted by someone who knows the child well; although this approach has many benefits, it also has downfalls.

Someone who knows the child well will know more about the child than someone who is an outside observer. They will be able to apply information they know from outside of the observation to understand what is happening during the observation, and they will know if what happens during the observation is typical of the child's behavior. An observer who knows the child, however, can also introduce observer bias. Observer bias occurs when observers interpret what they see through their own lens or perspective, which may not match the actual behavior being observed. A child's parent, caregiver, or educator may have trouble observing a child in an objective way. This may result in reports of the child's behavior that are more positive or more negative than an outside observer might report.

Observations can also be conducted by someone who does not know a child well (e.g., outside observer, researcher, school psychologist). An independent observer (someone who does not know the child) has the advantage of being able to observe the child without applying personal biases from his or her own experiences with the child. The downside to this is that independent observers can also impact a child's behavior. A child may be on his or her best behavior in the presence of a stranger or may exhibit more challenging behaviors than usual (e.g., throwing a tantrum) because the child is not comfortable in the presence of the observer. Either way, independent observers may not be able to determine on their own if the behavior they observe is typical or atypical for the child.

One way to reduce bias is through using a formal observation. Formal observations typically include a checklist, a rating scale, and/or a coding scheme that guides observers in what to look for and how to score their observations. Training for formal observations can be extensive in order to ensure that each observer is coding each child in the same way and that he or she is coding in the same way as other observers using the same measure. Examples of formal observations that measure aspects of children's self-regulation include the Observed Classroom Engagement Scale (OCES) (Rimm-Kaufmann et al., 2005) and the InCLASS (Downer, Booren, Lima, Luckner, & Pianta, 2010).

Formal observations can be very beneficial, especially for research purposes. Scores from formal observations can be used to compare children's skill levels across individual children and across groups of children and to measure growth over time. They can also be used to examine how a skill like self-regulation relates to other outcomes. For example, in one study, children's scores on the OCES predicted children's early reading skills (Ponitz, Rimm-Kaufman, Grimm, & Curby, 2009). In other words, children with higher scores on the OCES also had higher scores on reading assessments, suggesting a positive connection between self-regulation and reading skills. One limitation of formal assessments is that the required training may be time-intensive and expensive. The training, however, helps insure that the assessment is being used in a reliable way and in a way that minimizes bias.

Survey Data From Parents and Teachers

Educators and parents/caregivers are important sources of information about children's abilities, including self-regulation. There are numerous surveys that have been developed that provide questions related to self-regulation that parents/caregivers or educators can complete. Information obtained from a teacher and a parent/caregiver about a child's outcomes is likely to overlap in many ways; however, each also provides unique information about a child's self-regulation abilities from the different contexts in a child's life (e.g., at school versus at home, with peers versus with family members). Parents and caregivers know their children the best in the home environment and will be able to report on the role of self-regulation in the context of family life and sibling relationships. Teachers have extensive exposure to children in classroom settings and can report on the role of self-regulation at school as well as in the context of children's relationships with adults who are not family members and peers. One example of a widely used survey that assesses aspects of children's self-regulation is the Ages and Stages Questionnaire (ASQ) (Squires & Bricker, 2009). The ASQ is a series of parent- or caregiver-reported, age-graded developmental screening instruments (Squires & Bricker, 2009), and can be completed by parents or caregivers when children are between 2 and 60 months of age. An example of a teacher-rated measure of self-regulation is the Child Behavior Rating Scale (CBRS) (Bronson et al., 1995). The CBRS has been shown to significantly predict children's literacy and math skills in young children around the world (Schmitt, McClelland, Tominey, & Acock, 2015; von Suchodoletz et al., 2014; Wanless et al., 2011).

Just like informal observations, surveys can be subjective and may also be biased in some ways. Many studies have shown, however, that these survey ratings can be reliable, especially when the questions used are concrete and less open to individual interpretation. For example, asking teachers about children's ability to complete tasks and organize materials tends to be easier to report on than other aspects of behavior, such as if children have anxiety around peers. Like formal observations, survey scores can be used to compare children's abilities with one another, used to track growth, or used to examine relations with other related skills, like early academics. A number of studies have shown that teacher and parent surveys of children's self-regulation skills predict short- and long-term academic outcomes (Li-Grining, 2010; McClelland, Acock, & Morrison, 2006; McClelland et al., 2007; Sektnan, McClelland, Acock, & Morrison, 2010; von Suchodoletz et al., 2013; Wanless, 2011). For example, one study found that teacher ratings of self-regulation in the fall of kindergarten predicted children's academic achievement in reading and math skills between kindergarten and sixth grade (McClelland et al., 2006). These results were found in a diverse sample of children and even after taking into account the influence of important factors, such as children's intelligence, ethnicity, age, and parent education level. Another study using a large national dataset of nearly 1,300 children and families showed that parent ratings of children's self-regulation in preschool significantly predicted reading, math, and vocabulary skills at the end of first grade (Sektnan et al., 2010). In other words, children who have higher ratings on early self-regulation by parents and teachers are doing better than their peers on a range of outcomes, including achievement in reading and math through elementary school, middle school, high school, and college (McClelland, Acock, Piccinin, Rhea, & Stallings, 2013; Moffitt et al., 2011). One study even found that children who had strong attention abilities in preschool had nearly 50% greater odds of having completed college by age 25 than their peers (McClelland, Acock, Piccinin, Rhea, & Stallings, 2013).

Direct Assessments

Another way to measure children's self-regulation is through direct assessment. Direct assessment refers to measuring children's ability by giving them a task or test that they receive a score on. In early childhood, direct assessments are usually short activities or games aimed at measuring a specific skill. A few examples of direct assessments that measure self-regulation are the Dimensional Change Card Sorting (DCCS) task, the Attention Network task, and the Head-Toes-Knees-Shoulders (HTKS) task. The DCCS is a card-sorting task in which children are asked to sort a series of cards on different dimensions (e.g., size, color, or shape; Zelazo, 2006). The Attention Network task is a flanker task in which children must pay attention to an animal or object (e.g., a fish) on a computer screen and press a button corresponding to the direction that the fish is swimming in spite of distractor fish swimming in opposite directions on either side (Rueda, Rothbart, McCandliss, Saccomanno, & Posner, 2005). The HTKS is similar to Simon Says, but requires children to do the opposite of the request. For example, children are asked to touch their head when told to touch their toes. The HTKS has been gaining in popularity because children's scores on the HTKS consistently predict short- and long-term academic outcomes. The HTKS has been used in diverse groups of children in the U.S., Asia, and European countries (McClelland et al., 2007, 2014; McClelland & Cameron, 2012; Ponitz et al., 2009; von Suchodoletz et al., 2013; Wanless et al., 2011).

Using direct assessments with children has many benefits. One benefit is that scores from direct assessments tap into a child's ability and what a child can actually do rather than relying on information from others. What is amazing about this is that many of the direct assessments used with children are seemingly simple tasks (see Table 8.1); however, children's scores on many of these assessments are being shown to predict short- and long-term academic achievement (McClelland et al., 2007; Ponitz et al., 2009).

A limitation of direct assessments is that sometimes we are interested in knowing something about a child that it would be unethical to measure directly. For example, if we wanted to know how well and how quickly children are able to calm down after a temper tantrum, how would we measure that directly? Would we put children in situations that were designed to become increasingly frustrating until they experienced a meltdown or tantrum so that we could see what happens next? Absolutely not. It would probably be best to learn information like this from conducting observations in children's natural settings or surveying educators and parents. Another limitation of using direct assessments is that children can be unreliable test takers (Gullo, 2005). Giving a child a direct assessment on a day when the child is distracted and anxious to return to a fun activity in the classroom or when the child is not feeling well could result in a score that does not accurately measure the child's self-regulation abilities.

As we have discussed in this chapter, there are many reasons why early childhood educators might want to assess children's self-regulation abilities and many ways to do so. Although significant progress has been made in the field of self-regulation assessment, there is room for growth! Many existing measures have been designed for research purposes only. Educators may not have access to these assessments, and even if they do, they may not have a way to translate scores from these measures into classroom practices. The vast majority of assessments provide scores that are helpful in comparing children with their peers (e.g., seeing if a child is above or below average) or monitoring growth over time, but these scores are not accompanied by information related to how to turn them into strategies for improving children's self-regulation in the classroom. In spite of this, it is still important for educators to think about ways to assess children's self-regulation skills that support each individual child's needs and the needs of the class as a whole.

● ● ● ● ●

Learning Checkpoint #1

1. How is children's self-regulation typically assessed in your classroom or center? Are there formal assessments that are used (surveys, observations, or direct assessments) or informal processes?

2. What are the indicators that you look for when you think a child in your class might be struggling with self-regulation?

3. What support do you have available to you at your center if you need help during extremely challenging moments in the classroom?

●●●●●

Tips for Assessing Self-Regulation in the Classroom

1. *Increase your knowledge of self-regulation.* By reading this book (and seeking out other sources of information on self-regulation), you can build your knowledge of how self-regulation develops and how these skills typically look in the classroom. Having a solid knowledge base will help you know what to look for in children so that you have a sense of whether what you are observing is typical growth and development or indicative of self-regulation deficits and delays.

2. *Gather information from multiple sources.* No single assessment or observation can accurately capture a child's self-regulation abilities. Children's self-regulation development is shaped by many factors, including age, temperament, family, teachers and school experiences, socioeconomic status, culture, and more (McClelland, Cameron Ponitz, Messersmith, & Tominey, 2010). Gathering information from different sources can help paint a full picture of how a child's self-regulation abilities look across different contexts in the child's life (e.g., at school and at home) and the factors that are supporting or hindering growth in these skills. In addition to conducting your own observations of the children in your class, you may find it helpful to invite an outside observer to conduct an observation (e.g., an administrator at your school), and to have a conversation with the child's parents/caregivers about self-regulation at home, especially when you suspect a delay.

3. *Know your school's protocol for screening children and obtaining additional services and support.* Understanding your school's process for identifying children who need additional support or special services will help you access those supports when you need them. Children with severe difficulties are often identified first by teachers because of challenging behaviors exhibited in the classroom. Although protocols vary across programs, conducting observations is often the first step coupled with recording notes detailing evidence of delays or challenging behaviors. The next step often involves additional observations from school staff. Depending on a range of factors, the availability of support services varies widely. Regardless of whether outside support is needed, available, or obtained, teachers and administrators can work together to develop a plan to help

support children with self-regulation difficulties and help children practice and improve these skills.

4. *Ask for help and support when needed.* Even children who have not been identified as needing special services may require extra help and individual attention at times. In many early childhood classrooms, spending more than a few moments with an individual child is not possible. Speak with your co-teachers and administrators about ways to provide additional support for one another when challenging behaviors arise (e.g., having someone available to step in when an extra person is needed).

5. *Build your toolbox of self-regulation activities.* Having a wide range of activities and games that you can use throughout the day to promote self-regulation can help you promote growth and development for children at all levels of ability in your classroom, heading off future self-regulation challenges. Self-regulation practice can be embedded throughout the day in routines, during formal and informal learning activities, and in the language you use with children.

Reflect

What is one new thing you learned in this chapter about assessing children's self-regulation? How do you think this information can be helpful to you and your classroom?

Set a Goal

After reading the "Tips for Assessing Self-Regulation in the Classroom" section, identify one or more of the tips that would be helpful to you and your classroom.

● ● ● ● ●

Additional Resources

See Chapter 9 for additional resources related to the contents of this chapter, including Internet resources focusing on assessment in early childhood.

● ● ● ● ●

References

Achenbach, T. M., & Rescorla, L. A. (2000). *Manual for the ASEBA preschool forms & profiles: An integrated system of multi-informant assessment; child behavior checklist for ages 1 1/2–5; language development survey; caregiver-teacher report form.* University of Vermont, Burlington.

Bronson, M. B., Tivnan, T., & Seppanen, P. S. (1995). Relations between teacher and classroom activity variables and the classroom behaviors of preschool children in Chapter 1 funded programs. *Journal of Applied Developmental Psychology, 16*, 253–282. doi:10.1016/0193-3973(95)90035-7

Carlson, S. M. (2005). Developmentally sensitive measures of executive function in preschool children. *Developmental Neuropsychology, 28*(2), 595–616.

Cooper, D. H., & Farran, D. C. (1988). Behavioral risk factors in kindergarten. *Early Childhood Research Quarterly, 3*(1), 1–19.

Downer, J. T., Booren, L. M., Lima, O. K., Luckner, A. E., & Pianta, R. C. (2010). The Individualized Classroom Assessment Scoring System (inCLASS): Preliminary reliability and validity of a system for observing preschoolers' competence in classroom interactions. *Early Childhood Research Quarterly, 25*(1), 1–16.

Gullo, D. F. (2005). *Understanding assessment and evaluation in early childhood education.* New York, NY: Teachers College Press.

Kochanska, G., Coy, K. C., & Murray, K. T. (2001). The development of self-regulation in the first four years of life. *Child Development, 72*(4), 1091–1111.

LeBuffe, P. A. & Naglieri, J. A. (2012). *Devereux early childhood assessment for preschoolers* (2nd ed.). Lewisville, NC: Kaplan Early Learning.

Li-Grining, C. P., Votruba-Drzal, E., Maldonado-Carreño, C., & Haas, K. (2010). Children's early approaches to learning and academic trajectories through fifth grade. *Developmental Psychology, 46*(5), 1062–1077. doi:10.1037/a0020066

McClelland, M. M., Acock, A. C., & Morrison, F. J. (2006). The impact of kindergarten learning-related skills on academic trajectories at the end of elementary school. *Early Childhood Research Quarterly, 21*(4), 471–490.

McClelland, M. M., Acock, A. C., Piccinin, A., Rhea, S. A., & Stallings, M. C. (2013). Relations between preschool attention span-persistence and age 25 educational outcomes. *Early Childhood Research Quarterly, 28*(2), 314–324. doi:10.1016/j.ecresq.2012.07.008

McClelland, M. M., & Cameron, C. E. (2012). Self-regulation in early childhood: Improving conceptual clarity and developing ecologically valid measures. *Child Development Perspectives, 6*(2), 136–142. doi:10.1111/j.1750-8606.2011.00191.x

McClelland, M. M., Cameron, C. E., Connor, C. M., Farris, C. L., Jewkes, A. M., & Morrison, F. J. (2007). Links between behavioral regulation and preschoolers' literacy, vocabulary, and math skills. *Developmental Psychology, 43*(4), 947–959.

McClelland, M. M., Cameron, C. E., Duncan, R., Bowles, R. P., Acock, A. C., Miao, A. & Pratt, M. E. (2014). Predictors of early growth in academic achievement: The Head-Toes-Knees-Shoulders Task. *Frontiers in Psychology, 5*, 599. doi:10.3389/fpsyg.2014.00599

McClelland, M. M., Cameron Ponitz, C., Messersmith, E., & Tominey, S. (2010). Self-regulation: The integration of cognition and emotion. In R. Lerner (Series Ed.) & W. Overton (Vol. Ed.), *Handbook of life-span development: Cognition, biology and methods* (Vol. 1, pp. 509–553). Hoboken, NJ: Wiley.

Moffitt, T. E., Arseneault, L., Belsky, D., Dickson, N., Hancox, R. J., Harrington, H., . . . Caspi, A. (2011). A gradient of childhood self-control predicts health, wealth, and public safety. *Proceedings of the National Academy of Sciences, 108*(7), 2693–2698. doi:10.1073/pnas.1010076108

Ponitz, C., Rimm-Kaufman, S. E., Grimm, K. J., & Curby, T. W. (2009). Kindergarten classroom quality, behavioral engagement, and reading achievement. *School Psychology Review, 38*(1), 102–120.

Rimm-Kaufman, S. E., La Paro, K. M., Downer, J. T., & Pianta, R. C. (2005). The contribution of classroom setting and quality of instruction to children's behavior in kindergarten classrooms. *Elementary School Journal, 105*(4), 377–394.

Rueda, M. R., Rothbart, M. K., McCandliss, B. D., Saccomanno, L., & Posner, M. I. (2005). Training, maturation, and genetic influences on the development of executive attention. *Proceedings of the National Academy of Sciences, 102*, 14931–14936.

Schmitt, S. A., McClelland, M. M., Tominey, S. L., & Acock, A. C. (2015). Strengthening school readiness for Head Start children: Evaluation of a self-regulation intervention. *Early Childhood Research Quarterly, 30, Part A*(0), 20–31. doi:10.1016/j.ecresq.2014.08.001

Sektnan, M., McClelland, M. M., Acock, A., & Morrison, F. J. (2010). Relations between early family risk, children's behavioral regulation, and academic achievement. *Early Childhood Research Quarterly, 25*(4), 464–479. doi:10.1016/j.ecresq.2010.02.005

Smith-Donald, R., Raver, C. C., Hayes, T., & Richardson, B. (2007). Preliminary construct and concurrent validity of the Preschool Self-Regulation Assessment (PSRA) for field-based research. *Early Childhood Research Quarterly, 22*(2), 173–187.

Squires, J., & Bricker, D. (2009). *Ages and stages questionnaires: A parent-completed child-monitoring system* (3rd ed.). Baltimore, MD: Paul Brookes.

von Suchodoletz, A., Gestsdottir, S., Wanless, S. B., McClelland, M. M., Birgisdottir, F., Gunzenhauser, C., & Ragnarsdottir, H. (2013). Behavioral self-regulation and relations to emergent academic skills among children in Germany and Iceland. *Early Childhood Research Quarterly, 28*(1), 62–73. doi:10.1016/j.ecresq.2012.05.003

Wanless, S. B., McClelland, M. M., Acock, A. C., Cameron Ponitz, C., Son, S. H., Lan, X., . . . Li, S. (2011). Measuring behavioral regulation in four societies. *Psychological Assessment, 23*(2), 364–378. doi:10.1037/a0021768

Zelazo, P. D. (2006). The Dimensional Change Card Sort (DCCS): A method for assessing executive function in children. *Nature Protocols, 1*, 297–301.

9

• • • • •

Conclusions and Additional Resources

Now that you have reached the concluding section of our book, we hope that we have provided you with a practical resource that has extended your knowledge of research on self-regulation and provided you with a wealth of activities and ideas to expand your toolbox of strategies for promoting self-regulation in your classroom.

In this final chapter, we provide a "quick reference guide" for the tips and activities that were included in each chapter of this book as well as in the activity breaks so that you can easily find them when you need them (see Table 9.1). We also provide a list of additional

Table 9.1 Self-Regulation Tips and Activities by Chapter

Chapter	Self-Regulation tips and activities
1	**Self-Regulation in Early Childhood**
	• Tips for helping children learn to regulate intense emotions
2	**Laying the Foundation for Self-Regulation**
	• Tips for laying a foundation for self-regulation development
3	**Setting Up the Classroom for Self-Regulation Success**
	Activity Break #1: Circle Time Games to Promote Self-Regulation
	o Conductor*
	o It's Raining, It's Pouring
	o Introducing the Classroom Pet (Puppet)
	o Listening Bingo
	o Mirror, Mirror
	o Music Maps
	o Musical Simon Says
	o Mystery Bag
	o Sleeping, Sleeping, All the Children Are Sleeping*

(Continued)

Table 9.1 (Continued)

Chapter	Self-Regulation tips and activities
4	**Self-Regulation and Circle Time** o Ten tips for a well-regulated circle time **Activity Break #2: Supporting Circle Time Transitions Through Self-Regulation** o Do You Know My Friends? o Funny Faces Song* o Getting to Know You o If You're Wearing Blue Today o Jack Be Nimble o Let's See Who's At School Today o Let's Wave Our Hands and Sing Hello o Pass the Ball Around the Room o There Was a Boy/Girl Who Came to School
5	**Self-Regulation and Curriculum Areas: Literacy and Math** **Activity Break #3: Self-Regulation Games Promoting Literacy and Math** *Activities using self-regulation to promote literacy skills* o ABCs – Loud and Soft o Initial Consonant Simon Says o I Spy Something That Starts with "A" o Rhyme Time *Activities using self-regulation to promote math skills* o Counting by Twos o Matching Freeze Game o Number Hop o What's Missing?
6	**Integrating Self-Regulation Into Outdoor and Gross Motor Play** **Activity Break #4: Self-Regulation Games in Outdoor and Gross Motor Play** o Cooperative Freeze* o Drum Beats* o Freeze Dancing* o Red Light, Purple Light*
7	**Engaging Families in Self-Regulation Development** • Tips for effectively engaging families
8	**Self-Regulation Assessment and Intervention** • Tips for assessing self-regulation in the classroom
9	**Conclusions and Additional Resources** • Additional resources provided by chapter

*Games used in the Kindergarten Readiness Study.

resources corresponding with chapter topics, including links to articles on the Internet, recommended books for adults and children, and a list of intervention programs targeting self-regulation or aspects of self-regulation. The reference sections at the end of each chapter may also be a useful resource to help you identify research articles related to self-regulation.

Thank you for your taking the time to read our book and more importantly, thank you for all that you do to provide children with the skills they need (self-regulation and other), preparing them for social and academic success in early childhood and beyond.

●●●●●

Additional Resources for Chapter 1 (Self-Regulation in Early Childhood)

Internet Resources

"Cosmic Kids Yoga" www.youtube.com/user/CosmicKidsYoga

"Self-Regulation: The Second Core Strength" http://teacher.scholastic.com/professional/bruceperry/self_regulation.htm

Children's Books on Feelings, Managing Emotions, and Calming Strategies

The Chocolate-Covered-Cookie Tantrum
Author: Deborah Blumenthal
Illustrator: Harvey Stevenson
Publication Year: 1996
Publisher: Houghton Mifflin

The Great Big Book of Feelings
Author: Mary Hoffman
Illustrator: Ros Asquith
Publication Year: 2013
Publisher: Frances Lincoln Children's Books

Lots of Feelings
Author: Shelley Rotner
Publication Year: 2003
Publisher: Millbrook Press

On Monday When It Rained
Author: Cherryl Kachenmeister
Illustrator/Photographer: Tom Berthiaume
Publication Year: 2001
Publisher: Houghton Mifflin Sandpiper Books

The Quiet Book
Author: Deborah Underwood
Illustrator: Renata Liwska
Publication Year: 2010
Publisher: Houghton Mifflin

Quiet Loud
Author: Leslie Patricelli
Publication Year: 2003
Publisher: Candlewick

Sometimes I'm Bombaloo
Author: Rachel Vail
Illustrator: Yumi Heo
Publication Year: 2005
Publisher: Scholastic

Yoga Bear: Yoga for Youngsters
Author: Karen Pierce
Publication Year: 2004
Publisher: Cooper Square

You Are a Lion! And Other Fun Yoga Poses
Author/Illustrator: Tae-Eun Yoo
Publication Year: 2012
Publisher: Nancy Paulsen Books

Songs to Help Children Experience Feeling Calm

"Air on G String" by Johann Sebastian Bach
"Aquarium" from *Carnival of the Animals* by Camille Saint-Saëns
"Canon in D" by Johann Pachelbel

"Clair de Lune" by Claude Debussy

"Moonlight Sonata" by Ludwig van Beethoven

● ● ● ● ●

Additional Resources for Chapter 2 (Self-Regulation Development)

Internet Resources Focusing on Supporting Self-Regulation Development

"Building the Brain's 'Air Traffic Control' System: How Early Experiences Shape the Development of Executive Function" http://developingchild.harvard.edu/resources/reports_and_working_papers/working_papers/wp11/

"Developing Young Children's Self-Regulation Through Everyday Experiences" www.naeyc.org/files/yc/file/201107/Self-Regulation_Florez_OnlineJuly2011.pdf

"Key Concepts: Executive Function" http://developingchild.harvard.edu/key_concepts/executive_function/

"Self-Regulation: A Cornerstone of Early Childhood Development" www.naeyc.org/files/yc/file/200607/Gillespie709BTJ.pdf

"Taking Care of Yourself" www.naeyc.org/tyc/article/taking-care-of-yourself

● ● ● ● ●

Additional Resources for Chapter 3 (Setting up the Classroom)

Internet Resources Focusing on Integrating Self-Regulation in the Early Childhood Classroom

"Assessing and Scaffolding Make-Believe Play" www.naeyc.org/files/yc/file/201201/Leong_Make_Believe_Play_Jan2012.pdf

"Circle Time Puppets: Teaching Social Skills" www.naeyc.org/files/tyc/file/V4N4/Circle_time_puppets_teaching_social_skills.pdf

"Helping Children Make Transitions Between Activities" http://csefel.vanderbilt.edu/resources/wwb/wwb4.html

"Moving Right Along: Planning Transitions to Prevent Challenging Behavior" www.imagineeducation.com.au/files/CHC30113/BTJ_20Moving_20Right_20Along_20Planning_Transitions.pdf

Recommended Children's Books Focusing on Self-Regulation

From Head to Toe
Author: Eric Carle
Publication Year: 1997
Publisher: HarperFestival

How Do Dinosaurs Play With Their Friends?
Author: Jane Yolen
Illustrator: Mark Teague
Publication Year: 2006
Publisher: Blue Sky Press

My Friend and I
Author: Lisa Jahn-Clough
Publication Year: 2009
Publisher: Houghton Mifflin

Waiting Is Not Easy
Author: Mo Willems
Publication Year: 2014
Publisher: Disney-Hyperion

● ● ● ● ●

Additional Resources for Chapter 4 (Circle Time)

Internet Resources Focusing on Self-Regulation Activities and Games

"Enhancing and Practicing Executive Function Skills With Children From Infancy to Adolescence" http://developingchild.harvard.edu/resources/tools_and_guides/enhancing_and_practicing_executive_function_skills_with_children/

"Self-Regulation Activities" www.yourtherapysource.com/selfregulation.html

"Self-Regulation in the Classroom: Games and Exercises" https://self-regulationintheclassroom.wikispaces.com/Games+and+Exercises

Early Childhood Intervention Programs Targeting Self-Regulation

Al's Pals www.wingspanworks.com

Chicago School Readiness Project http://steinhardt.nyu.edu/ihdsc/csrp

Collaborative for Academic, Social, and Emotional Learning (CASEL) www.casel.org/guide

I Can Problem Solve www.researchpress.com/books/590/icps-i-can-problem-solve

The Incredible Years Series www.incredibleyears.com

Kids in Transition to School (KITS) www.oslc.org/projects/kids-transition-school-kits/

Kindergarten Readiness Study www.selfregulationlearning.com

Peaceworks: Peacemaking Skills for Little Kids www.peace-ed.org

Preschool RULER http://ei.yale.edu/ruler

Promoting Alternate Thinking Strategies (PATHS) www.pathstraining.com

Responsive Classroom www.responsiveclassroom.org

Second Step www.cfchildren.org/second-step

Tools of the Mind www.toolsofthemind.org

● ● ● ● ●

Additional Resources for Chapter 5 (Math and Literacy)

Internet Resources Focusing on Early Literacy and Math

"Early Childhood Mathematics: Promoting Good Beginnings" www.naeyc.org/files/naeyc/file/positions/psmath.pdf

"The Essentials of Early Literacy Instruction" www.naeyc.org/files/tyc/file/Roskos.pdf

"Everyday Steps to Reading and Writing" http://families.naeyc.org/everyday-steps-to-reading-writing

"Math Talk with Infants and Toddlers" http://families.naeyc.org/learning-and-development/music-math-more/math-talk-infants-and-toddlers

"Support Math Readiness Through Math Talk" http://families.
naeyc.org/learning-and-development/music-math-more/
support-math-readiness-through-math-talk

"Support Math Readiness Through Music" http://families.
naeyc.org/learning-and-development/music-math-more/
support-math-readiness-through-music

"Whatever Happened to Developmentally Appropriate Practice in
Early Literacy?" www.naeyc.org/files/yc/file/200507/02Neuman.
pdf

* * * * *

Additional Resources for Chapter 6 (Outdoor/Gross Motor Play)

Internet Resources Focusing on Outdoor and Gross Motor Play

"Big Body Play: Why Boisterous, Vigorous, and Very Physical Play Is
Essential to Children's Learning and Development" www.naeyc.
org/store/files/store/TOC/241.pdf

"Taking Movement Education Outdoors" www.naeyc.org/files/yc/
file/201107/LeapsAndBounds_OnlineJuly2011.pdf

"Why Motor Skills Matter" www.naeyc.org/files/yc/file/200807/
BTJLearningLeapsBounds.pdf

Recommended Children's Books Focusing on Outdoor and Gross Motor Play

Are You Ready to Play Outside?

Author: Mo Williems

Publication Year: 2008

Publisher: Disney-Hyperion

* * * * *

Additional Resources for Chapter 7 (Engaging Families)

Internet Resources Focusing on Engaging Families

"Family Participation in Decision Making and Goal Setting" www.
naeyc.org/familyengagement/principles/1

"Getting Parents 'Ready' for Kindergarten: The Role of Early Childhood Education" www.hfrp.org/publications-resources/browse-

our-publications/getting-parents-ready-for-kindergarten-the-role-of-early-childhood-education

"Reciprocal Relationships" www.naeyc.org/familyengagement/principles/3

"Research News You Can Use: Family Engagement and Early Childhood Education" www.naeyc.org/content/research-news-family-engagement

"Two-Way Communication" www.naeyc.org/familyengagement/principles/2

Internet Resources Focusing on Promoting Self-Regulation at Home

"Building Social and Emotional Skills at Home" http://families.naeyc.org/learning-and-development/child-development/building-social-and-emotional-skills-home

"Helping Your Child Begin Developing Self-Control" www.zerotothree.org/child-development/social-emotional-development/teaching-your-child-discipline-and-self-control.html

"Help Your Child Become a Great Problem-Solver" http://families.naeyc.org/child-development/help-your-child-become-great-problem-solver

"Readiness: Not a State of Knowledge, but a State of Mind" http://families.naeyc.org/learning-and-development/music-math-more/readiness-not-state-knowledge-state-mind

"Setting Limits: Helping Children Learn Self-Regulation" www.pbs.org/wholechild/parents/building.html

"Vroom Parenting Tools and Activities" www.joinvroom.org/tools-and-activities

"What Parents Need to Know About Supporting Self-Regulation" www.toolsofthemind.org/parents/self-regulation/

Recommended Self-Regulation Books to Build Your Parent Library

How to Talk So Kids Will Listen & Listen So Kids Will Talk
Authors: Adele Faber and Elaine Mazlish
Publication Year: 2012
Publisher: Scribner

Mind in the Making: The Seven Essential Life Skills Every Child Needs

Author: Ellen Galinsky

Publication Year: 2010

Publisher: Harper Collins

Parenting From the Inside Out

Author: Daniel Siegel and Mary Hartzell

Publication Year: 2013

Publisher: Tarcher

Peaceful Parenting, Happy Kids: How to Stop Yelling and Start Connecting

Author: Laura Markham

Publication Year: 2012

Publisher: Perigee Books

The Whole-Brain Child: 12 Revolutionary Strategies to Nurture Your Child's Development

Authors: Dan Siegel and Tina Payne Bryson

Publication Year: 2012

Publisher: Random House

Recommended Children's Books to Support Secure Child and Family Relationships

Guess How Much I Love You

Author: Sam McBratney

Illustrator: Anita Jeram

Publication Year: 2008

Publisher: Candlewick Press

The Kissing Hand

Author: Audrey Penn

Illustrators: Ruth Harper and Nancy Leak

Publication Year: 1993

Publisher: Tanglewood Press

● ● ● ● ●

Additional Resources for Chapter 8 (Measuring Self-Regulation)

Internet Resources Focusing on Assessment in Early Childhood

"Choosing an Appropriate Assessment System" www.naeyc.org/files/yc/file/200401/shillady.pdf

"Early Childhood Curriculum, Assessment, and Program Evaluation" www.naeyc.org/files/naeyc/file/positions/CAPEexpand.pdf

"What Do I Say to Parents When I Am Worried About Their Child?" www.earlychildhoodnews.com/earlychildhood/article_view.aspx?ArticleID=208

Index •••••